Y0-BQT-451

MOTHERS AND MOTHERING

WOMEN'S HISTORY AND CULTURE
(VOL. 3)

GARLAND REFERENCE LIBRARY
OF SOCIAL SCIENCE
(VOL. 646)

WOMEN'S HISTORY AND CULTURE

1. *Feminism and Women's Issues: An Annotated Bibliography and Research Guide*
   G. Llewellyn Watson

2. *The Indian Captivity Narrative: A Woman's View*
   Frances Roe Kestler

3. *Mothers and Mothering: An Annotated Feminist Bibliography*
   Penelope Dixon

MOTHERS AND MOTHERING
An Annotated Feminist Bibliography

Penelope Dixon

GARLAND PUBLISHING, INC. • NEW YORK & LONDON
1991

Library of Congress Cataloging-in-Publication Data

Dixon, Penelope, 1948–
Mothers and mothering : an annotated feminist bibliography / Penelope Dixon
p. cm. — (Women's history and culture ; 3) (Garland reference library of social science ; vol. 646)
Includes index.
ISBN 0–8240–5949–2
1. Mothers—United States—Bibliography. 2. Motherhood—United States—Bibliography. 3. Feminism—United States—Bibliography. I. Title. II. Series. III. Series: Garland reference library of social science : v. 646.
Z7963.M67D59 1991
[HQ759]
016.306874'3—dc20 90–24981
CIP

Printed on acid-free, 250-year-life paper
Manufactured in the United States of America

This book is dedicated to the possibility of mothering that exists within all of us; more specifically, it is for the three of us: Edna, Penelope and Emily.

CONTENTS

ACKNOWLEDGMENTS

I would like to thank the following institutions and persons for helping make this book a reality: The Graduate Center, City University of New York, for allowing me to submit the core of this work as the thesis for my Master's Degree in Liberal Studies; The New York Public Library for providing a desk in the Wertheim study room; The Schlesinger Library at Harvard for its superb database on women's studies and the help of its librarians; Merran Kavanagh for her research help as well as her typing and proofreading of innumerable copies of the manuscript, all in good spirit; Cheryl Finley and Alex Chisholm for their research work; Marie Ellen Larcada for her editorial and emotional support as well as the other staff at Garland who have been involved with getting this book out of the computer and onto the printed page; and last, but certainly not least, my husband, Michael Ball, for his unending encouragement and belief in what I needed to do.

FOREWORD

All of us, at least at some point in our lives, are affected by mothering. The importance of this issue is reflected in the amount of research that has been done in the past two decades on various aspects of the subject. Single-parent families, career women, reproductive technologies and abortion are all topics that are concerned with women's mothering. The issue of mothering is of great concern to feminist writers from a variety of disciplines, including sociology, psychology, anthropology and literature. Besides numerous individual articles, this can be evidenced by whole issues of journals such as *Feminist Studies* (4:2), *Frontiers* (3:2), *Women's Studies Quarterly* (11:4), *Hypatia* (1:2), *Sage* (1:2) and *Journal of Marriage and the Family* (34:3), which have been devoted to the subject.

My purpose in compiling this annotated bibliography and collection of review essays is to try and separate the various sub-topics relating to mothering as analyzed by feminists, and then offer a selection of this information. I have divided the literature into the following categories: mothers and mothering, mothers and daughters, mothers and sons, single mothers, working mothers, lesbian and black mothers, mothering and the family, children, feminism, psychoanalysis and reproductive issues as they relate to mothering.

To create the annotated bibliography sections of this book, I searched existing bibliographies, particularly those in the works by Miriam Johnson, Judith Arcana, Ann Dally, David Lynn, Beverly Birns and Dale Hay, Paula Caplan and Jean Curtis, among others. Useful bibliographies pertaining to specific categories are mentioned in the introductory essays to each section. The extensive bibliographies written by Judith Barker[1] and Sue Walters[2] for their doctoral dissertations were also of great help. Next, I searched the New York

Public, City University of New York and Schlesinger (Harvard) libraries for books on mothering and related subjects such as the family and children. Finally, I conducted a search through the indexes of *Women's Studies Abstracts* from 1980 through the present for relevant journal material. An initial database search of the psychological and sociological abstracts offered little relevant material, although I suspect a physical search might find additional articles.

There is not room here for everything that has been written on the subject. I have chosen to include, with a few exceptions, articles and books written since 1970. I have annotated many of the books published during this period, along with a selection of the journal literature.

The amount of journal literature on the subject of mothering is immense. I have included a sampling but there are many additional articles of which the potential researcher should be aware. Some are narrowly focused, such as studies on black teen-age mothers, others are in difficult-to-locate publications, such as *Plexus*, *Women's Studies International Forum*, *Atlantis* and *Belles Lettres*. Some articles have been done as part of later books which are annotated herein; when the article is particularly important, I have annotated it separately. Two aspects of the journal literature which I have tried to include are studies that provide a review, with authors' names and dates, of recent articles on the subject and review essays of recent books.

One new area of research which has resulted in a plethora of books and articles in recent years is that of surrogacy and reproductive technologies; I have included selected works in this area, although an entire bibliography on the subject could be created.

Areas which I have chosen not to include in this book are historical and fictional entries, "how-to" (be a successful single parent, etc.) books, cross-cultural studies, except for a small sampling, psychological literature on mother-infant relations, books on childbirth and pregnancy. Due to their lack of easy access, masters' theses and dissertations have not been included, although much useful research has been done in these media.

With the exception of one new book by Nan Bauer Maglin and Nancy Schneidewind, research on stepmothers is most often found in the abundance of divorce literature, some of which is covered here. Black studies and works on lesbians are only cursorily covered, as many references on mothering are included in general books on these cultures and are too numerous to include here. The same holds true for disabled mothers, although *The Different Faces of Motherhood* by Birns and Hay does include a chapter and list of references on this subject. Only a sampling of European books and articles have been reviewed, most of which are from Britain. Finally, articles in popular magazines, including *Ms.* have not been included although it should be noted that *Ms.*, in particular, has had a number of good articles relating to mothering over the past 15 years.

The majority of writers whose works have been reviewed herein note that they have one particular viewpoint: primarily that of a white, middle-class, heterosexual feminist. These writers also usually point out that they have/have not taken into consideration the effects of cross-cultural, ethnic, class and racial factors in their research. My point of view is that of a feminist working mother. All mothers work but within the limits of this book I use the term "working mother" to refer to mothers who work at paid employment.

In order to assist the potential researcher I have cross-referenced certain works between sections, i.e., a book which has been annotated under the single mothers section but which also contains pertinent information on black mothers has been cross-referenced between the two sections. I also use the notation "see . . ." or "(. . .)" to refer the reader to various other entries in the bibliography that pertain to the entry at hand.

Notes

1. Barker, Judith. "Single Mothers, Powerlessness and Empowerment: A Class, Race and Sexual Orientation Comparison." Dissertation presented to the Department of Sociology, University of Oregon, 1989.

2. Walters, Sue. "Mothers and Daughters in Popular Culture." Dissertation presented to the Department of Sociology, City University of New York, 1989.

Mothers and Mothering

I.

Mothering Today: A Brave New World

Mothering is a feminist issue. Some feminists, such as Jeffner Allen (1) and Shulamith Firestone (305), have tried to dismiss the role of mothering on the premise that mothers at home with children are supporting patriarchy. Other women who are full-time mothers and consider themselves feminists, complain that the women's movement has denigrated their choice (see Elaine Heffner, 49, and Lydia O'Donnell, 70). Working mothers, who represent the great majority of women today, treat their careers and mothering as equally important roles in their lives. The result is a proliferation of books and articles about mothering written in the past two decades from a variety of feminist and non-feminist perspectives. This work reviews the former.

The major works by Nancy Chodorow, Dorothy Dinnerstein, Adrienne Rich and Miriam Johnson have a common thread: the institution of motherhood is the root cause of oppression for women. They also agree that gender roles are sociologically, not biologically, created. A separation of childbearing from childrearing removes the biological basis from mothering and the availability of day care defeats the functionalist argument, i.e., it is not necessary for the woman to stay at home, as a sexual division of labor is no longer needed. Finally, the instinctual argument that women "need" to mother or that babies "need" their own mother all of the time has been debunked (Chodorow, *Reproduction of Mothering*, 19, p. 23).

Therefore, it follows that mothering is a product of feminine role-training and identification. Sara Ruddick points out in *Maternal Thinking* (81) that certain features of the mothering experience are invariable, such as gestation and infant dependence whereas others are alterable while remaining universal. Childbearing results in childrearing and women usually become the caretakers, often dependent on the fathers.

Although they are both parents, there are many differences between mothers and fathers. As Rich notes, women know themselves both as daughters and potential mothers beginning at an early age and continuing through their forties. Men, on the other hand, know themselves as sons, and only much later, as potential fathers (Rich, *Of Woman Born*, 76, p. 118). According to Rich, the inclination of most women to have children is still considered a secondary sex-characteristic whereas men's desire for a family appears to stem from societal conditioning. And even so, men's fathering as a social role is less constant than women's mothering.

How does society's view of the family and woman's place within it influence mothering today? The pronatalist forces who believe that women's primary role is in being a mother put tremendous pressure on women. This pressure can be either blatant, as in the anti-abortion movement, or extremely subtle. Media images of mothers and children coupled with negative portrayals of career women work together to convince women of the "right" choice.[1] Relations between women, men and children are not fixed by biology but, rather, are socially organized by institutions, ideology and roles.

Johnson's important work, *Strong Mothers, Weak Wives* (54), looks more to society than the mother herself as the cause of women's acceptance of male dominance. She argues that both genders learn nurturant qualities from their experience of being mothered but males later deny this experience as the result of participation in adolescent male peer groups. She also blames the father for encouraging anti-female behavior in the son. Boys are socialized by their families and their peers to be involved in active, and sometimes violent play. They are seldom found playing with dolls.

There are many questions concerning mothering that need to be addressed. How does the fact that women have always mothered affect the fact of their mothering today? This is one of the main issues that Chodorow addresses. Chodorow was one of the first to write on the subject and subsequently has authored more books and articles than any other feminist writer, nine of which are annotated in this bibliography.

She believes that the mother-daughter relationship results in the female psyche and that women mother because of this psychological character formation. This she calls the reproduction of mothering. Chodorow argues that all people, men and women, should have the relational basis for parenting since they were parented themselves. The fact remains that it is primarily women who fulfill the needed caretaking responsibilities for children. This, Chodorow believes, is because the relationship between a mother and daughter differs from that between a mother and son. In the former, relational possibilities are extended, whereas in the latter they are curtailed. This is essentially the same point that Johnson makes, just from a different perspective.

It is also the main theme of Carol Gilligan's work and Gilligan acknowledges Chodorow's influence on her thinking (Gilligan, *In a Different Voice*, 324, p. 7). Chodorow posits that because of their mothering by women, girls feel less separate and define themselves more in relation to others. "The basic feminine sense of self is connected to the world, the basic masculine sense is separate" (*The Reproduction of Mothering*, 19, p. 169). This is the basis on which society functions.

Chodorow's work has naturally evoked criticism, even within the feminist community. Pauline Bart (5), Robert Gottleibe (45), Judith Lorber and Alice Rossi (60) all criticize Chodorow's analyses for being embedded in psychoanalysis rather than current social structures while Marcia Westkott (131) accuses her of a lack of context with regards to patriarchy. Patriarchy can be defined as

> . . . the power of the fathers: a familial-social, ideological, political system in which men—by force, direct pressure, or through ritual, tradition, law, language, customs, etiquette, education, and the division of labor, determine what part women shall or shall not play . . . (Rich, *Of Woman Born*, p. 59)

Chodorow does, in fact, state that "women's mothering is a central and defining feature of the social organization of gender and is implicated in the construction and reproduction of male dominance itself" (*The Reproduction of Mothering*, p. 9).

The relation of mothering to patriarchy should not be ignored. The patriarchal society in which we live needs women to act as mothers for its survival. If women gain total control of reproduction, they will destroy at least some of the basis of the patriarchal order. This is why issues such as surrogacy and technological innovations surrounding pregnancy are so important. Phyllis Chesler and Barbara Katz Rothman, among others, have recently addressed these concerns.

Many other authors are concerned with mothering and its perpetuation of patriarchy, including Jeffner Allen (1), Jessie Bernard (9), Stephanie Dourick (28), Diane Ehrensaft (31), Ann Oakley (69) and Betsy Wearing (87) in this section as well as Shulamith Firestone (305), Simone de Beauvoir (301) and Jill Lewis (118) whose works are annotated in later sections. Although it is agreed that current-day mothering perpetuates patriarchy, there are differing opinions as to how this takes place and as to the best solution for change. Dinnerstein (27), and Chodorow in her early works (100, 300), have a tendency to blame the mother herself for producing the foundations of male dominance through her mothering. They acknowledge that this mothering takes place within patriarchy yet they, and particularly Dinnerstein, still lay responsibility with the mother. Chodorow, in her article with Susan Contratto (21), has started to move away from this myth of the all-powerful mother.

The viewpoint espoused by Rich, Bernard and others is that the institution of motherhood, not mothers themselves, is responsible for male dominance and the patriarchy. Lewis notes that the isolation within marriage, inferior legal and economic status and cultural images which praise femininity while disempowering women are the material conditions in which women mother (*Common Differences*, 118, p. 131). The nuclear family of the absent-father and involved mother sets the stage for the continuation of male dominance within the greater bounds of society.

If we accept that either of these premises, i.e., women's mothering or the institution of dependent motherhood, is responsible for contributing to the propagation of patriarchy, then we must look for solutions. One early idea espoused by certain feminists, including Allen, Firestone and de Beauvoir, was that equality for women and an end to patriarchy could only be achieved by the abandonment of mothering. Rich, Bernard and Ehrensaft, who feel that altering the conditions, as opposed to an elimination of mothering, is the proper course of action, offer a more contemporary outlook.

Many feminists have claimed that full-time mothering is harmful to both mothers and children, as well as to society. "The idea of healthy adults giving all of their energies to a few healthy children is a cultural anomaly," states Sara Ruddick in her introduction to *The Mother Knot*

(58), p. xiv. The low self-esteem of many full-time mothers, as noted by Mary Boulton (11), is a reflection of the low status attributed by society to childcare. Both Boulton and Bernard point out that some women may need this role to establish their femininity and respectability but that their own development as adults will eventually suffer and they will remain second-class citizens. A few authors such as Elaine Heffner (49) and Shirley Radl (75), who agree that full-time mothering can be a problem for the mothers, still feel that it is the best situation for the children.

This obviously does not make sense. An unhappy mother is not going to produce happy, well-adjusted children. Another major repercussion for the children is sex-role stereotyping, which is admirably addressed by Sandra Bem in her article on raising gender-aschematic children (283). Mothers at home and fathers at work reinforce the concept of current gender roles. In her interviews with mothers and daughters, Anita Shreve (223) found many daughters who saw their working mothers as role models and attached prestige to having a mother with an interesting career.

It is not just that full-time mothering is harmful to society because it perpetuates male dominance which will eventually lead to the destruction of the world, at least according to Dinnerstein in *The Mermaid and The Minotaur* (27), p. 4. One must look also at the loss of labor, of intellect and nurturance which society suffers as a result of women working full-time as mothers and housewives.

Heffner, Lydia O'Donnell (70) and Jean Bethke Elshtain (269) see full-time mothering as a viable choice. Their work has been included because it is important to understand this opinion which is still espoused by a large portion of young women. O'Donnell considers herself a feminist and insists that full-time mothering can be a contribution which benefits all aspects of society.

Shared parenting is one possible solution to the problem of full-time mothering which many theorists including Chodorow, Dinnerstein and Virginia Held (50) advocate. They feel that it will address the problems of role stereotyping for the children and development of the mother's identity as separate from the child. Jessica Benjamin (316) suggests that shared parenting could offer the possibility for change but also feels that male attitudes of domination could be reproduced through men parenting. This is also Johnson's fear of shared parenting, that the very system which needs to be destroyed will be encouraged.

Ehrensaft has actually studied the reality of shared parenting and found that it is problematic within the current patriarchal system. Males are not socialized to be parents and most workplaces do not offer well-paid part- or flex-time jobs. According to Sanford Matthews and Maryann Brinley (63) the *right* part-time work is the solution to the problems caused by full-time mothering. Charlene Canape, author of *The Part-Time Solution: The New Strategy for Managing Your Career While Managing Motherhood* (New York: Harper & Row, 1990), would apparently agree.

There are many other issues concerning mothering which are explored in this section. Susan Contratto (23), Ann Ferguson (38) and Ronnie Friedland and Carol Kort (39) look at the little-studied concept of maternal sexuality while Shelia Kitzinger (55) and Leigh Minturn (66) investigate mothers in different cultures to see what is universal and what varies. The relatively new concept of delayed motherhood wherein women are choosing careers over mothering, at least until well into their childbearing years, is the subject of two books: *Up Against the Clock* (35) by Marilyn Fabe and Norma Wikler and *The Biological Clock* (209) by Molly McKaughan and the issue of multiple roles for women, i.e., spouse, parent, worker is the concern of numerous writers in the section on working mothers. Finally, mothers in transition: from daughters to mothers, from wives to single parents, from full-time homemakers to workers and students has been studied by many of the authors including Vangie Bergum (7), Pamela Eakins (29), Lucy Fischer (105) and Matthews and Brinley (63).

Other sub-classifications of mothers that do not have entire sections devoted to them in this bibliography include mothers in prison (see 6, 295), mothers without custody (see 30, 46, 76, 157, 250), disabled mothers (see 10, 392), and stepmothers (see 61).

All of this current activity on the issue of mothering and its importance both in relation to women's growth and the continuation of patriarchy has inevitably resulted in a backlash of opinion. Other writers like Bruno Bettelheim[2] and Selma Fraiberg[3] insist that only women can provide adequate mothering for their children. Authors such as these are well read and subsequently influence a great deal of society. They should not be ignored if we wish to address a wider audience than those of us already dedicated to feminist principles and the destruction of patriarchy. As Rich has wisely said, "There is one taboo that has withstood all the recent efforts at demystification: the idealization of motherlove" (*Of Woman Born*, p. 279).

Notes

1. Goffman, Erving. *Gender Advertisements*. New York: Harper & Row, 1979.

2. Bettelheim, Bruno. *A Good Enough Parent: A Book on Child-Rearing*. New York: Knopf, 1987.

3. Fraiberg, Selma. *Every Child's Birthright: In Defense of Mothering*. New York: Basic Books, 1977.

BIBLIOGRAPHY—MOTHERING TODAY

1. Allen, Jeffner. "Motherhood: The Annihilation of Women" (1982) in Joyce Trebilcot, ed. *Mothering: Essays in Feminist Theory*. Totowa, N.J.: Rowman & Allanheld, 1984, pp. 315–330.

Allen offers a radical analysis of motherhood as dangerous to women through its continuation of patriarchy by the introduction of both boy and girl children into the world of men. Allen sees women's abandonment of mothering as the only means to freedom. Certain other feminists that Allen quotes, de Beauvoir (301), Firestone (305), etc., also adhere to this view. This essay is an interesting contrast to the more familiar views of mothering by Dinnerstein and Chodorow as a means to changing the world.

2. Badinter, Elizabeth. *The Myth of Motherhood: An Historical View of the Maternal Instinct*. London: Souvenir Press, 1981.

Originally published in France as *L'Amour en plus*, Badinter's thesis is that the "maternal instinct" is not innate, but is learned through social conditioning. She gives, as an historical basis, a history of childrearing practices in eighteenth century France wherein a majority of children were given up by their parents. Badinter sees this as evidence of a survival instinct which overrides a maternal one. She compares these women to contemporary mothers who choose, as opposed to it being a financial necessity, to return to demanding jobs soon after the birth of their children. Francine du Plessix Gray's foreword to this edition gives a critical review of Badinter's work, putting her in the context of French feminist tradition as exemplified by de Beauvoir and comparing and contrasting her to Rich's (76) views of motherhood. This book has also been published in the United States under the title *Mother Love*. This is an important European work which should be read in conjunction with the major American books by Rich, Dinnerstein (27) and Chodorow (19).

3. Barber, Virginia, and Merrill M. Skaggs. *The Mother Person*. Indianapolis: Bobbs-Merrill, 1975.

The two authors interviewed over 50 women, including one single mother by choice, about the effect of becoming a mother on their lives. The purpose of the book is to dispel the myths of motherhood and offer a realistic picture of childrearing for women contemplating having a baby or already involved in the experience of mothering. One important point the authors make is that choosing not to have children is a more benign selfishness than deciding to give birth to one's own. Although somewhat an advisory or "self-help" book which contains much of the authors' own experience as mothers, it offers an early enlightened, if not exactly feminist, look at the realities of motherhood and the need for solidarity among women. In some ways, this is a lay book of the far more political *Of Woman Born* (76) published a year later. The authors correctly note that (in 1975) there are few books which address the problems of the mother as a person in her own right, but rather are concerned with the development of children.

4. Bart, Pauline. "The Mermaid and the Minotaur, a Fishy Story That's Part Bull." *Contemporary Psychology* 22 : 11 (1977): 834–835.

Bart's scathing review of Dinnerstein's *The Mermaid and the Minotaur* (27) is of "a book whose time has gone." She points out that Dinnerstein blames the present problems of our world on the fact that children are raised by mothers alone, while neglecting to see that mothers are operating without any real power in a patriarchal society. She also castigates Dinnerstein for ignoring the effects of mothering on the mothers themselves and for bringing up the idea of female masochism. Although harsh, Bart's review is fair, particularly in the light of more current feminist research. See also Bart's review (5) of Chodorow's *The Reproduction of Mothering*, as well as Snitow's (3) review of Dinnerstein's work.

5. Bart, Pauline. "Review of Chodorow's *The Reproduction of Mothering*" (19) in Joyce Trebilcot, ed. *Mothering: Essays in Feminist Theory*. Totowa, N.J.: Rowman & Allanheld, 1984, pp. 147–152.

   Bart's comment that "Chodorow has written a book on motherhood that few mothers can read" is fair since the book was not written with only the lay person in mind. Her critique that Chodorow bases her theories solely on sessions with psychoanalytic patients, rather than direct observations of mothers and children is accurate. She sees Chodorow and Dinnerstein (see 4, above, Bart's review of Dinnerstein) as both attributing problems between genders to a result of women's mothering and offering a solution of bringing men into the picture. Bart shows how this is in contrast to the writings of Rich (76), Arcana (92) and Westkott (131). The general tone of this review is sarcastic and appears to contain a certain amount of academic jealousy. Bart complains that certain negative reviews of Rich's *Of Woman Born* were hatchet jobs done by women, while doing precisely the same thing herself in this review, which was first published in *Off Our Backs* 11: 1 (January 1981). Bart has written another piece on mothering, "The Loneliness of the Long-Distance Mother," published in the second edition of Jo Freeman's *Women: A Feminist Perspective*, which was unavailable for annotation.

6. Baunach, Phyllis Jo. *Mothers in Prison*. New Brunswick, N.J.: Transaction Books, 1985.

   Although the literature concerned with the separation of inmate-mothers and children consistently recommends programs to maintain ties, there has been little research documenting the background, development, implementation or perceived success of these programs, according to Baunach. Her objectives in this study were first, to provide descriptive analyses of such programs, second, to explore imprisoned mothers' perceptions of the effects of separation from their children on themselves and on their children and third, to investigate the roles and perceptions of foster parents in relation to the incarcerated mothers. Since this was an exploratory study, Baunach does not offer any concrete conclusions but rather suggests certain hypotheses for further testing, such as: most mothers consider the separation as temporary and have retained legal custody; mothers want to maintain ties and do so through letters, telephone calls and visits; many mothers noted that the separation exacerbated or caused problems in the children. In this regard see Stanton (295) for a study of the effects of incarceration of mothers on their children.

7. Bergum, Vangie. *Woman to Mother: A Transformation.* Granby, Mass.: Bergin & Garvey, 1989.

As the title of this work suggests, Bergum is concerned with the transformation of women into mothers through the processes of pregnancy and birth. Writing as a feminist, Bergum incorporates the experiences of six women from their decisions to have a child through the birth with well-documented references to a variety of authors, including many who have been reviewed in this bibliography. The conclusions she reaches are that the decision to have a child is incredibly complex and not necessarily rational. She sees childbirth as a sexual experience by which women are irrevocably changed. She also believes that the responsibility of becoming a mother belongs to women themselves, as opposed to medical personal or government agencies. See Matthews and Brinley (63), Fischer (105) and Eakins (29) for other works on transition.

8. Bernard, Jessie. *The Future of Motherhood.* New York: Dial Press, 1974.

Bernard's concern is with the institution of motherhood as it is informed by certain traditions, beliefs and symbols, etc. that have been shaped by technological, political, economic and ethical forces. This pre-dates Rich's work on motherhood as both an experience and institution; it is notable that Rich does not credit Bernard in *Of Woman Born* (76) for these ideas. Bernard sees the reintegration of the roles of mother and worker as one of the major priorities today. She is one of the first writers to look at the role of mothers as it relates to women themselves, rather than to their children. Much of what Bernard has written is still relevant today such as her concern with the various technologies relating to motherhood and her repudiation of the maternal instinct as being too socialized to be instinctual.

9. Bernard, Jessie. *Women, Wives and Mothers: Values and Options*. Chicago: Aldine, 1975.

   Bernard sees full-time mothering as imposing restrictions on the development of women as individuals, resulting in their remaining second-class citizens. She also sees contemporary mothering as having dire repercussions on children in terms of sex-role stereotyping. In contrast to Heffner (49), Bernard finds that there are mothers who, although they love their children, dislike the experience of motherhood. Her ideas are similar to those of Rich (76), particularly the chapters "Mothers in Transition." "Policy-Relevant Research on Motherhood" and "Adolescence and Socialization for Motherhood."

10. Birns, Beverly, and Dale Hay, eds. *The Different Faces of Motherhood.* New York: Plenum Press, 1988.

   The editors, both developmental psychologists, set out to learn more about the differences in mothers, who are basically treated generically in terms of their relationships to infants and young children. They note that if we believe a child's early years are vitally important, we must understand more about the mother. Their idea in seeking contributions from a variety of professionals (all women) was to reflect current scholarship in a range of disciplines as well as to generate hypotheses. Some of the areas covered include divorced mothers, delayed motherhood, disabled mothers, black mothers and major theories of mothering including sociobiological and psychoanalytical. Each section has a useful bibliography included. The section on disabled mothers, a rarity in the literature, offers many insights such as the prejudice of researchers in regards to the parenting abilities of the disabled and the support these women felt from their roles as mothers (see Arditti et al., 332, for another reference to disabled mothers.) The section on black mothers includes an historical account, a review of the current literature and a comparison to the lives of white mothers including the startling fact that twice as many black mothers and children die in childbirth as compared to white.

11. Boulton, Mary Georgina. *On Being a Mother: A Study of Women with Pre-School Children*. New York: Tavistock Publications, 1983.

    Boulton's thesis is that biological mothers who are entirely responsible for their children, as their *only* responsibility, are unique to Western industrialized society. She reviews a number of studies of mothers and children in a variety of journals and offers the conclusion that mothers who mother exclusively are often so frazzled by the experience that they are unable to nurture their children. Boulton sees the influence of social networks as a positive experience for mothers (see Bilge and Kaufman 146, Brown 150, Weiss 174 and Smith 173 for similar viewpoints) and finds a correlation between women with rewarding careers and good mothering. This book, originally written as Boulton's doctoral thesis, is based on interviews with 50 mothers.

12. Brans, Jo, and Margaret Taylor Smith. *Mother, I Have Something to Tell You*. Garden City, N.Y.: Doubleday, 1987.

    This book offers a journalist's account based on a research study of "highly traditional" mothers whose children have chosen or grown into "unexpected," "untraditional" and/or "unacceptable" lifestyles (as judged by the mothers). The writer and researcher note that through six distinct stages (shock, attention, action, detachment, autonomy and connection) most of the mothers changed and grew in reaction to their children's lifestyles, which included everything from alcoholism to homosexuality. The authors conclude that such experiences encourage (if only by force) a positive process of ego separation which might not otherwise have occurred. The book seems aimed primarily at mothers who might include themselves among this diverse group. Almost no information on the study itself is included.

13. Burck, Frances Wells, ed. *Mothers Talking: Sharing the Secret.* New York: St. Martin's Press, 1986.

    Burck states that the goal of her book is to celebrate motherhood and honor its importance. To accomplish this she has interviewed, without using questionnaires, numerous women about the experience of motherhood. Forty-two of these women speak for themselves on topics ranging from adoption to working mothers to "motherhood burnout." Although not particularly feminist in content, many of the statements are insightful and honest concerning the difficulties of mothering while showing a good understanding of its meaning to many women's lives.

14. Burton, Linda, Janet Dittmar and Cheri Loveless. *What's a Smart Woman Like You Doing at Home?* Washington, D.C.: Acropolis Books, 1986.

    These three women, who began by publishing a newsletter for mothers who choose to stay at home, aim to dispel stereotypes of this lifestyle. Based on unsolicited letters (in response to radio, press and television appearances) their thesis is that the majority of women, if given the choice, would choose to stay at home over other options. This is a rich sample of experiences (although it is impossible to know the backgrounds of the women since the letters are unsolicited) but it is difficult to get past the impression that they are all drawn from the same pool. The book succeeds in showing us that a wide range of women are happy at home, but it is not convincing that all or most women find homemaking to be, as one woman puts it, "the most important thing we can do for mankind." Despite what some readers will interpret as backlash bias, the authors do offer a subtle look at this group of women who make their lives at home.

15. Caine, Lynn. *What Did I Do Wrong? Mothers, Children, Guilt.* New York: Arbor House, 1985.

Caine writes a personal narrative of motherhood from the perspective of a widow raising two children. She is particularly concerned with the insidious mother-blaming which is practiced by society in general as well as by mothers themselves. Her conclusion, after conducting her own informal research through interviews and questionnaires, is that mothers only have a limited amount of influence over their children, be it good or bad. Caine notes that the best thing she feels she did for her own children was presenting them with a women who had diverse interests and abilities, of which mothering was but one.

16. Chesler, Phyllis. *With Child: A Diary of Motherhood.* New York: Crowell, 1979.

Written as a journal from the beginning of her pregnancy in May 1977 through January 1978, Chesler describes her feelings about becoming a mother late in life, and in mid-career. She looks at how her pregnancy affects her relationships with her unborn daughter, her mother, her friends and her colleagues. This is a personal account, poetically written, about the conflicts of mothering. Chesler's pregnancy and the birth of Chesler's child hurt her academically as she was forced to give up teaching because her university refused to give her a flexible schedule which would allow her to take care of her daughter, as well as continue her academic career.

17. Chesler, Phyllis. *Mothers on Trial: The Battle for Children and Custody*. New York: McGraw-Hill Book Co., 1986.

This is a large book (over 600 pages), indexed with a list of resources for battered women, mothers in prison, child support and custody needs. There are also extensive notes to all the chapters. *Mothers on Trial* deals with the question of "good enough" mothering and what happens when mothers are challenged for the custody of their children. Chesler points out that the standards for good enough mothering are based on gender, race, class and religion. Good enough mothering can evidently best be done by educated white women staying at home with their children. Like all of Chesler's books, this one is accessible as she uses first hand accounts from women she meets in her therapy practice and intersperses this with news stories of public figures and various statistics. The perspective is historical as well as cross-cultural.

18. Chodorow, Nancy. "Mothering, Object-Relations, and the Female Oedipal Configuration." *Feminist Studies* 4: 1 (1978): 137–158.

    The contents of this article are basically incorporated in Chodorow's work, *The Reproduction of Mothering* (19), which was published in the same year. Chodorow extends her thesis that the female psyche results from the mother-daughter relationship and that this relationship contributes to the creation of male dominance. She interprets the *feminine* oedipus complex as being a mother-daughter, rather than a father-daughter, issue because women, not men, mother. The father-daughter relationship can only be understood in the context of the ongoing relationship of the daughter to her mother. Chodorow goes on to explore the "feminine sense of self-in-relationship" which Carol Gilligan uses as the basis of her different voice. This article offers a good synopsis of Chodorow's complex theories.

19. Chodorow, Nancy. *The Reproduction of Mothering: Psychoanalysis and the Sociology of Gender*. Berkeley: University of California Press, 1978.

    Chodorow's thesis is that women mother not because it is a natural instinct or because of gender-role formation (Dinnerstein, 26) nor because of ideology (Rich, 76) but because of psychological character formation. Women cannot be forced to mother well but do so because they have the capacity and choose to use it. Chodorow uses object-relations theory to trace infant development through "good enough" mothering to the subsequent reproduction of this mothering in female children. Girls experience a different set of relational experiences with the mother than do boys which results in the female possessing a greater "relational potential." *The Reproduction of Mothering* is occasionally contradictory and repetitive with some psychoanalytical terminology, but over all it is well researched and scholarly. See Bart (5), Eisenstein (34), Gottleibe (45),

Haaken (47), Hirsch (114), Lewis (118), Lorber (60), Raymond (53) and Westkott (131) for critiques of this work.

20. Chodorow, Nancy. "Mothering, Male Dominance and Capitalism" (1978) in Zillah R. Eisenstein, ed. *Capitalist Patriarchy and The Case For Socialist Feminism.* New York: Monthly Review Press, 1979, pp. 83–106.

    Basically containing similar ideas to those found in *The Reproduction of Mothering* (19), this chapter was written near the time of that publication. It focuses on Chodorow's theme that mothering, as it is practiced in the current patriarchy, is responsible for male dominance and the continuation of capitalism which depends, in part, on women's unpaid labor. Chodorow concludes that women's position is not biologically determined, but can be changed by a reorganization of parenting. She critiques Rossi's (278) goals of returning parenting to the center of social organization as ignoring the fact that women's mothering is central to the reproduction of the patriarchy.

21. Chodorow, Nancy, and Susan Contratto. "The Fantasy of The Perfect Mother" (1980) in Barrie Thorne, ed. *Rethinking the Family: Some Feminist Questions.* New York: Longman, 1982, pp. 54–75.

    The authors thoroughly review, critique and compare various contemporary writings on mothering including Firestone (305), Dinnerstein (27), Arcana (92), Flax (106), Rich (76), Lazarre (58) and Rossi (278), among others. They see as a recurrent theme the idea that mothers are often held totally responsible for their children's development, regardless of patriarchal society's influence. Mother-blaming and idealization of the mother themes can be found in *both* traditional and feminist writing. The authors conclude that many feminist writers have connected a child-centered perspective with a myth of maternal omnipotence and perfection which makes victims of both the mother and child. They feel that the relationships of parenting and gender can only be transformed by moving beyond these myths. As long as mothers are treated as all-powerful or powerless, we deny the complexity of their lives. This essay has also been published in

Chodorow's recent book, *Feminism and Psychoanalytic Theory* (318).

22. Comer, Lee. *Wedlocked Women*. Leeds: Feminist Books, 1974.

Written during the beginning years of the Women's Liberation Movement in Britain, Comer attempts to analyze the subjection of women in their family roles of housewife and mother. The section on motherhood includes a number or early insights into the mystique of motherhood, such as full-time mothering being unhealthy for both mother and child (see Bernard, 9). She also points out that studies on the effects of maternal deprivation were often studies of institutionalized childcare. Many of these ideas are, of course, elucidated by later writers such as Rich (76). This book is concisely written and full of references to early 1970s publications.

23. Contratto (Weisskopf), Susan. "Maternal Sexuality and Asexual Motherhood." *Signs* 5: 4 (1980): 766–782.

Contratto defines maternal sexuality as a woman's sexual feelings while she is involved in the tasks of mothering and asexual motherhood as a cultural belief that mothers are not and should not be sexual persons. She points out that there is little research on the subject of maternal sexuality because of the anxiety and guilt associated with behaviors and feelings which are considered taboo. She feels that many women have internalized the identity of the asexual mother which painfully conflicts with their real feelings. This is a fascinating article which looks at psychoanalytic and biosocial theories and the reproductive cycle of women with the conclusion that the fragmentation of women's sexual and mothering experiences must be corrected, both in research and in reality. See *Hypatia* (53) for a number of essays on this subject.

24. Dally, Ann G. *Mothers: Their Power and Influence*. London: Weidenfeld and Nicolson, 1976.

This book is based on the author's personal observation of mothers seen during the course of her psychiatric practice. Dally has observed three types of mothers (which are similar to three stages of mothering): a mother that stresses enclosure, one that stresses extension and the third who stresses separation. Children who do not experience the initial stage of enclosure have later problems of vulnerability and lack of self-esteem while those who are excessively controlled never develop independence and authenticity. Satisfactory extension results in a harmony with the outside world for the child; the problems of this stage are discussed by Alice Miller (291) in relation to narcissistic cathexis. According to Dally, separation is the ultimate achievement for the mother and child; Gilligan (324), of course, challenges this stress on separation. Dally believes that one can predict which type a woman will be by studying her childhood and through psychological observations. The emphasis is on adult children and how they can make the best of the mothering they have received. See Caplan (96) and Fischer (105) for other works with the same emphasis and (24) for Dally's more recent work.

25. Dally, Ann G. *Inventing Motherhood: The Consequences of an Ideal*. London: Burnett Books, 1982.

Dally, who is a practicing psychiatrist and mother of six, concentrates on the psychological rather than the social aspects of mothering. She sees present-day motherhood as a crisis for women who stay home, burdened with an idealized picture of motherhood, caring for their children in isolation. She believes that women should combine mothering with outside work or at the very least, with community networks. Dally looks at mothering today including the positive effects of feminism on ideas concerning mothering; she includes a brief history of mothering and a good bibliography with a variety of British references and historical books on mothering.

26. Davitz, Lois Leiderman. *Baby Hunger: Every Woman's Longing for a Baby*. Minneapolis: Winston Press, 1984.

Questionnaires and interviews with 200 women are the basis of Davitz's thesis that *all* women, at one point in their lives, experience an "instinctual, overpowering drive" to have a baby. She supports her thesis largely with anecdotes and uses the diversity of her sample as evidence that baby hunger is an inevitable, biological phenomenon. She gives a breakdown of the marital status of study participants, and says that the sample was balanced in terms of race and class. It is assumed that all participants are heterosexual. Half theory, half self-help, her book suggests that women's acceptance of the reality of baby hunger is the key to wholeness, whether or not they choose motherhood.

27. Dinnerstein, Dorothy. *The Mermaid and The Minotaur: Sexual Arrangements and Human Malaise*. New York: Harper & Row, 1976.

The Mermaid and the Minotaur investigates how our present day "gender arrangements," i.e., the activities and roles of men and women, came to be and why they appear to be so difficult to change. Dinnerstein's thesis is that women's mothering is the main reason that our planet is endangered by humans who are unable to live in harmony with themselves and their environment. Being taken care of by a woman, insufficiently, according to Dinnerstein, is the infant's first experience which affects her/him for life. Dinnerstein fails to take into account that no mother can attend to her child's needs 100% of the time; in fact, if she does, the child will never attain the necessary self-confidence to become an independent individual. Dinnerstein feels that for men, this mothering results in hatred and fear of women and a need to control them; for women, there is not the same fear of losing the mother as they become the mother themselves. The only solutions, according to Dinnerstein, is for men to participate in childrearing and for the integration of a woman-centered perspective into world politics. This complex book offers many controversial ideas, many of which bear consideration. See Bart (4), Chodorow and Contratto (21), Eisenstein (33), Gottleibe (45), Haaken (47), Hirsch (114), Raymond (53) and Snitow (3) for critiques of this work.

28. Dourick, Stephanie, ed. *Why Children?* New York: Harcourt Brace, 1980.

This is a collection of essays on mothering written by 18 women from various continents, primarily living in England, many who have chosen not to mother and most of whom write from the political left. Dourick's essay looks at motherhood inside patriarchy from the viewpoint of a revolutionary committed to overthrowing the current social order. She believes that one can mother from outside patriarchy by remaining involved in the world through work and social commitments. Also included is an essay by Sara Ruddick (see 80, 81) who talks about raising an adolescent son and daughter and her experience of being a wife, mother and writer within a parochial academic community similar to the situation described by Jane Lazarre (58). This collection is very personal, with the pieces by mothers showing the struggle to retain one's selfhood in the midst of parenting while those by non-mothers are encouraging for others who have chosen not to parent.

29. Eakins, Pamela S. *Mothers in Transition: A Study of the Changing Life Course*. Cambridge, Mass.: Schenkman, 1983.

This book looks at an unusual group of women: mothers returning to college after having dropped out to become full-time homemakers. Despite the resistance of families and friends, as well as their own inner doubts, most of these women were successful in obtaining degrees and many noted the psychological rewards of discovering their individual selves, apart from their roles of mother and homemaker. Eakins also looks at returning homemakers who dropped out before completing their degrees due to family pressures and their own lack of confidence in their work. Most of these women suffered from a period of depression. The author blames the re-entry programs of colleges for not being realistic in terms of the needs of these women while setting them up for traditional jobs based on policies which are formed by sexism and ageism. She also points out that marriage can be disfunctional for women as it often does not encourage them to develop as individual people. See Bergum (7), Fischer (105) and Matthews and Brinley (63) for other studies on transition.

30. Edwards, Harriet. *How Could You? Mothers Without Custody of Their Children.* Freedom, Calif.: Crossing Press, 1989.

Based on over 100 questionnaires and interviews, as well as a review of the literature, Edwards examines the variety of experiences of women who, for lack of a better term, she calls non-custodial mothers. She came to this research from her own experience: having left her husband and children, she wondered how many other women had made comparable choices, and how they felt about them. The result is a very dense exploration of a group of women who defy categorical analysis but who have a lot in common. Some have involuntarily lost custody through divorce proceedings, while others have left willingly, sharing custody on paper but functioning as absentee parents. Despite the differences, Edwards is able to weave the voices together with her own authentic one in a way that does not diminish the richness of the individual experiences. This is a very readable book written in a tone of dedicated inquiry, making it illuminating to the researcher and inspiring to anyone involved in one of these complex situations. It ends with an excellent annotated bibliography that even includes a list of related and helpful fiction for children. See Greif (46) and Paskowicz (71) for other studies on non-custodial mothers.

31. Ehrensaft, Diane. "When Women and Men Mother" (1980) in Joyce Trebilcot ed. *Mothering: Essays in Feminist Theory.* Totowa, N.J.: Rowman & Allanheld, 1984, pp. 41–61.

Ehrensaft believes that a reorganization of parenting has become a necessity due to the lack of traditional nuclear families, e.g., single parents and two-worker families. This gives the left (feminist) an advantage over the right (pro-life) who want to maintain the patriarchy which is based, in part, on the one-worker nuclear family. Like various other feminist writers including Dinnerstein (27) and Chodorow (19), Ehrensaft sees shared parenting as a means to eliminating sex-gender roles. She analyzes the experiences of a small group of parents who have attempted shared parenting to see both the potential and actual effects. She finds the reality of shared parenting to be problematic within the capitalist system; there appears to be a void between the political potential and the actual limitations due to, in part, the socialization of males. This is an interesting look at what happens when we follow the advice of Chodorow and Dinnerstein. This article is an excerpt from an essay originally published in the *Socialist Review* 49 (January/February 1980).

32. Eisenstein, Hester. "The Cultural Meaning of Mothering: I. As Experience and Institution" (1980) in *Contemporary Feminist Thought*. Boston: G.K. Hall, 1983, pp. 69–78.

    This chapter by Eisenstein is an analysis of Rich's *Of Woman Born: Motherhood as Experience and Institution* (76). It starts with an overview of early feminist literature concerning reproduction and mothering including such names as de Beauvoir, Firestone and Rossi which leads up to Rich's work in 1976. Eisenstein explains Rich's distinction between the female "experience" of motherhood and the male dominated "institution" and gives a good synopsis of Rich's thesis that motherhood itself is not the means by which women are enslaved but rather the way it is set up in patriarchal society. It is a good introduction to Rich's complex work.

33. Eisenstein, Hester. "The Cultural Meaning of Mothering: II. The Mermaid and the Megamachine" (1980) in *Contemporary Feminist Thought*. Boston: G.K. Hall, 1983, pp. 79–86.

    This chapter by Eisenstein is an analysis of Dinnerstein's *The Mermaid and the Minotaur* (27). Eisenstein offers a synopsis of Dinnerstein's book with some critique of Dinnerstein's thesis that women's mothering is the cause of the "human malaise" threatening our planet. She explains Dinnerstein's analysis of gender arrangements as the means by which women's and men's activities and roles are divided on the basis of gender alone, i.e., women give birth so therefore, women mother. Eisenstein compares Dinnerstein to Rich (76), giving Rich's theories a more favorable view, particularly in terms of mothers and daughters. Rich sees the separation of the mother and daughter as the "essential female tragedy" whereas Dinnerstein states that women don't need their mothers since they become the mother themselves. As in Eisenstein's analyses of Rich (32) and

Chodorow (34) her chapter on Dinnerstein is a well-written and lucid synopsis of a complex book as well as a viable critique of Dinnerstein's theories.

34. Eisenstein, Hester. "The Cultural Meaning of Mothering: III. The Construction of Gender Identity" (1980) in *Contemporary Feminist Thought*. Boston: G.K. Hall, 1983, pp. 87–95.

This chapter by Eisenstein is an analysis of Chodorow's *The Reproduction of Mothering: Pyschoanalysis and the Sociology of Gender* (19). Although it is primarily a synopsis of Chodorow's theories as outlined in *The Reproduction of Mothering*, Eisenstein goes on to raise questions about Chodorow's lack of incorporation of lesbian mothers and the relation of mothers with only male children to her theories. She ties Chodorow's ideas into those of other writers such as Firestone (305) and Dinnerstein (27) which is useful in looking at these various theories about motherhood. She gives a succinct explanation of Chodorow's complex object-relations theories.

35. Fabe, Marilyn, and Norma Wikler. *Up Against the Clock: Career Women Speak on the Choice to Have Children*. New York: Random House, 1979.

Fabe and Wikler have combined the personal accounts of ten women with interviews of 75 others, all of whom deferred the decision whether or not to have children into their thirties. The authors' purpose was to help undecided women, including themselves, resolve their minds about motherhood, a dilemma which is caught up in a turmoil of political, social, biological and emotional issues. They found three main reasons why many women are either waiting to or undecided about having children: (1) they don't know what effect a child would have on their careers and vice versa; (2) the only way to have a child was to be a single mother and what are the consequences on the child and the self; (3) they don't think they want a child but are worried about what they might be missing. After establishing these concerns, the authors concluded there were not viable resources to help women make this decision and felt the best resource would be the experiences of other women which they have incorporated in this book and which they hope will suggest new ways of resolving these conflicts. See McKaughan (209) and Wilk (227) for other books on this subject as well as a chapter in Birns and Hay (10).

36. *Feminist Studies.* Special Issue: Towards a Feminist Theory of Motherhood. 4: 2 (Summer 1978).

    In her introductory essay, "Washing Blood," Rachel Blau du Plessix states that this is not a practical issue with essays on child-care and parenting but rather that it includes the poetics of discovery. The issue includes poems, prose, photographs, literary criticism, historical pieces and a few "practical" articles which have been annotated here separately, see Flax (106) and Snitow (3).

37. Ferguson, Ann. "On Conceiving Motherhood and Sexuality: A Feminist Materialist Approach" (1982) in Joyce Trebilcot, ed. *Mothering: Essays in Feminist Theory*. Totowa, N.J.: Rowman & Allanheld, 1984, pp. 153–182.

    Written from the viewpoint of a feminist social theorist, Ferguson looks at the continuation of male dominance as a result of two cross-cultural constants: women's ability to become biological mothers and the fact that most children are "mothered." She investigates whether the differing consequences of male and female sexuality and the division of parental labor also perpetuate this dominance. Ferguson takes into consideration that the relations of motherhood and sexuality vary in different societies, at different historical periods and depend on race and class. This work may be difficult for the non-academic reader but it offers an important analysis which differs, according to Ferguson, from the "static, deterministic emphasis of feminist neo-Freudian analyses like those of Nancy Chodorow" (p. 176). See Ferguson's later works on motherhood and sexuality (37, 324).

38. Ferguson, Ann. *Blood at the Root: Motherhood, Sexuality, and Male Dominance*. London: Pandora, 1989.

Ferguson offers a new feminist theory which connects motherhood, sexuality, male dominance and economics. Part I includes critiques of theories of social dominance which examine radical feminist, Marxist, Freudian and socialist-feminist theories. Part III, which is concerned with feminist politics, includes a chapter on contemporary motherhood. This chapter includes a critique of many of the writers annotated herein: Chodorow, Gilligan, Allen, Ruddick, Flax, Rich, Joseph, etc. Ferguson believes that motherhood cannot be considered the basis for a superior female ethic but rather that there should be alternative feminist countercultural family forms which restructure male-female relationships. This work contains an extensive bibliography. See the special issue of *Hypatia* on motherhood and sexuality which was edited by Ferguson (53) and includes an essay by her (234).

39. Friedland, Ronnie, and Carol Kort, eds. *The Mothers' Book: Shared Experiences*. Boston: Houghton Mifflin, 1981.

Interspersed with photographs and a few poems, this book consists of writings by mothers on pregnancy, postpartum experiences, working, staying at home, sexuality in motherhood, single mothering (including one mother who gave up custody), adoption and step-mothering. The purpose of the editors, both of whom are mothers, was to find out from other women what it feels like to be a mother today. They have uncovered a wide range of experiences, most of which dispel the "super woman myth" and include feelings of ambivalence regarding mothering (see Genevie and Margolies, 40, for the same findings). Examples of this ambivalence include the problems of parenting a gifted child, a formerly abused child's ability to mother and the issue of mother-daughter rivalry.

40. Genevie, Louise, and Eva Margolies. *The Motherhood Report: How Women Feel About Being Mothers*. New York: Macmillan, 1987.

Genevie looks at the myth and reality of motherhood, through the stages of pregnancy, childbirth and child-raising, with chapters on mothers and daughters, mothers and sons, single and working mothers. It is based on a survey of 870 North American mothers conducted by National Family Opinion, Inc. to see how they felt about being mothers. Most felt that their expectations of motherhood were "a far cry from the way it really is" and many were ambivalent about their experiences (see Friedland and Kort, 39). The questionnaire is included in the appendix; some of the questions are qualitative, some factual, some essay. The whole effect is similar to the *Hite Report*. Each section is primarily made up of quotes with comments and analysis by the authors from a fairly objective and, if any bias, feminist point of view. It is not a survey of particularly feminist families, as most of the mothers were indulging in sexist child raising and most of the single mothers bemoaned the lack of a father, but the authors are aware enough of feminist politics to note this aspect of the study.

41. Gerson, Mary-Joan, Judith L. Alpert and Mary Sue Richardson. "Mothering: The View from Psychological Research." *Signs* 9: 3 (1984): 434–453.

The authors begin by noting that until recently the study of mothering in psychological literature reflected the absence of a feminist consciousness. Rather it focused on the relation between childrearing practices and child development. Feminist research, however, is primarily concerned with how motherhood may, or may not, be instrumental for women in realizing their personal goals; this is reflected in more current psychological literature with an interest in the major life experiences that differentiate the lives of men and women. The authors look at demographic trends as evidenced by U.S. government statistics and then study the role of motherhood as a series of the developmental stages identified by Rapoport and Strelitz (218). They conclude that present public policy as it relates to mothering is clearly entrenched in traditional values. An effort to separate parenting responsibilities from gender-specific roles should be encouraged and the well-being of both parents and children taken into consideration. Three other articles by Gerson (42, 43, 307) are annotated in this bibliography as well as Alpert's book on women and psychoanalysis (313).

42. Gerson, Mary-Joan. "Feminism and the Wish for a Child." *Sex Roles* 11: 5/6 (1984): 389–397.

Gerson investigated the motivations for parenthood in 184 unmarried, childless, female college undergraduates and found that positive memories of early childhood maternal love, traditional feminine sex-role identification and anti-feminist beliefs are the primary psychological variables accounting for the wish to have children. Feminism, defined in the study in terms of receptivity to and approval of feminist goals, was found to be negatively related to the motivation for motherhood by a number of researchers besides Gerson. The various measures used in this study are interesting in themselves such as the Index of Parenthood Motivation which consists of six components including the ranking of childrearing relative to other adult activities and the rating of overall benefits and costs of having children. It was found that although women who subjectively identify with feminism are less interested in becoming mothers, those feminists who did express the desire for a child saw motherhood as offering opportunities for mastery and assertiveness. Therefore, the costs of childrearing for feminist women appear to center on a loss of freedom with regard to career aspirations. Gerson also points out that the positive motivation for parenthood related to happy childhood memories is inversely related to feminism, i.e., women with feminist sympathies often do not have positive memories of their mothers in early childhood. An earlier version of this article was published as "The Lure of Motherhood" (*Psychology of Women Quarterly*) 5: 2 Winter 1980: 207–217. See Gerson's other articles (41, 43, 307).

43. Gerson, Mary-Joan. "The Prospect of Parenthood for Women and Men." *Psychology of Women Quarterly* 10: 1 (1986): 49–62.

This study of 113 men and 75 women between the ages of 21 and 42 is an extension of Gerson's earlier study on parenthood motivation in young women (42) as particularly related to feminism. In this study feminism was eliminated as a significant variable, perhaps, according to Gerson, because older women are better able to integrate career ambition with the wish for a child.

Age was significantly related to motivation with younger men and women expressing a greater desire for children even though the "biological clock" is ticking louder for older subjects. The results of this present study indicate that for women, psychological variables such as narcissism, self-esteem and memories of father's love have a much stronger relationship to parenthood motivation than do demographic variables such as socioeconomic status, age and marital status. The wish for a child reflects very different patterns of identity structure in males and female and for women, the decision of whether to become a parent emerges from the complex structure of personality and identity rather than from more external and sociologically based variables.

44. Gordon, Tuula. *Feminist Mothers.* New York: New York University Press, 1990.

Gordon looks at how women with alternative ideologies and theories, such as feminism, construct their lives within the cultures of our present-day society and what possibilities as well as limitations they find. Rather than considering motherhood in isolation, she integrates it with other aspects of women's lives. She starts off by looking at the process whereby girls are socialized into femininity. She has interviewed 25 women including black, lesbian, single, middle and working-class. Gordon believes that since feminism emphasizes that women are strong and have rights, feminist mothers should be able to develop critical orientations toward social structures and cultures, including the motherhood myth. This book includes a thorough bibliography with many British references. It was originally published in London by Macmillan.

45. Gottleibe, Roger. "Mothering and the Reproduction of Power: Chodorow, Dinnerstein, and Social Theory." *Socialist Review* 14: 5 (1984): 93–119.

This essay focuses on Chodorow and Dinnerstein's claims that women's mothering is responsible for the oppression of women. Gottleibe acknowledges their contributions to theories of gender but states that their arguments rest on two incorrect assumptions:

psychological dispositions determine human behavior and that individuals are best understood from their experience as infants. He also says that there is a difficulty in explaining society as a whole by early experiences of the individual and that it is important to realize there are many collective interests, such as all the male-dominated institutions, which have an interest in perpetuating mothering. Gottleibe believes that mothering would not be reproduced if children entered a non-sexist society after initial upbringing by women.

46. Greif, Geoffrey L., and Mary S. Pabst. *Mothers Without Custody*. Lexington, Mass.: Lexington Books, 1988.

For the purpose of this study, non-custodial mothers are defined as those mothers who spend eight nights or less per month with their child or children. The authors found that of the 100 mothers interviewed, one half of whom gave up custody voluntarily, one third were content with the situation, one third were ambivalent and one third were unhappy. A significant difference was noted between attitudes toward non-custodial fathers and mothers—the former is viewed as the norm and is applauded for any involvement or support whereas the mother is considered unfit if she has lost custody or unnatural if she has given it up, regardless of the fact that non-custodial mothers spend more time than non-custodial fathers with their children. The book includes a good reference section on custody and family issues as well as numerous statistical tables. Mothers with split custody (not having custody of a least one child) describe themselves as less involved with the children living away and felt less guilt. The way the custody arrangements were arrived at impacted on the mothers' adjustment. The biggest differences between non-custodial fathers and mothers were: finances, guilt feelings and reactions of outsiders. See Paskowicz (71) and Edwards (30) for other studies on non-custodial mothers.

47. Haaken, Janice. "Freudian Theory Revised: A Critique of Rich, Chodorow, and Dinnerstein." *Women's Studies Quarterly* II: 4 (Winter 1983): 12–15.

Haaken's focus is on the use of psychoanalytic theory in feminist teaching as exemplified by the works of Chodorow (19), Dinnerstein (27) and Rich (76) on mothering. She finds that although psychoanalysis may provide a coherent theory for understanding certain subjective dimensions of mothering, it has the potential for being too far removed from social realities. Haaken's essay goes on to explain her own method of teaching from a psychoanalytic-feminist approach and then offers a comparison of Chodorow's, Dinnerstein's and Rich's approaches from this same theoretical perspective. She notes that while all three are concerned with the reproduction of sexual inequality, Rich dismisses psychoanalytic theory while simultaneously using it and Dinnerstein is defensive about her ideas which do address this theory's potential value. Haaken is most supportive of Chodorow's object relations theory and feels that Chodorow's critical explication of the potential value of psychoanalysis to feminism is a major contribution to feminist scholarship.

48. Hare-Mustin, Rachel T., and Patricia C. Broderick. "The Myth of Motherhood: A Study of Attitudes Toward Motherhood." *Psychology of Women Quarterly* 4: 1 (Fall 1979): 114–128.

These authors developed the Motherhood Inventory (MI), a 40-item questionnaire which studied attitudes toward motherhood and the motherhood myth in 301 college students and their parents. Attitudes toward reproductive control, adoption, single motherhood and punitive aspects relating to the myth of motherhood are compared in informative tables by age, gender, religious preference and education. Women were generally found to be more liberal than men. Most issues that divided men and women on the MI were found to be concerned with power and decision-making, and more males than females tended to agree with the statement that the mother-child relationship is the essential human relationship. Younger and unmarried subjects appeared to agree more with the myth of motherhood, but this was probably due to the fact that most of these were Catholic. The most significant differences related to education, generally those with less education supported the "myth of motherhood."

49. Heffner, Elaine. *Mothering: The Emotional Experience of Motherhood after Freud and Feminism.* New York: Doubleday, 1978.

Heffner's book focuses on the emotional experience of motherhood as it has been affected by psychoanalytic theory and the women's movement. She accuses the women's movement of trying to liberate mothers from mothering rather than helping them become successful mothers and says that a full-time commitment to raising children is a professional choice. Although Heffner may be correct in saying that mothering is humanizing (everyone should do it, not just women) and that it takes special skills, she fails to point out that it is not necessarily a full-time activity nor is this activity a full-time choice for most mothers. This book is essentially a backlash against feminist theories of mothering (see O'Donnell, 70, for a similar view) yet is important to look at in the context of contemporary writing on the subject during the last decade.

50. Held, Virginia. "The Obligations of Mothers and Fathers" (1979) in Joyce Trebilcot, ed. *Mothering: Essays in Feminist Theory.* Totowa, N.J.: Rowman & Allanheld, 1984, pp. 7–20.

Held writes along the same lines as Dinnerstein (27) and Chodorow (19) that the only way to provide for the continuation of humanity is for men to share in parenting, as exclusive mothering by women results in male dominance which is responsible for putting the planet at risk. This article primarily deals with the question of equality in parenting roles. Held looks for an answer within the given social conditions of the United States and decides that all tasks to do with children should be divided equally, and not on the sex of the parent. This theoretical view is somewhat problematic, as many children are being raised by single mothers yet the author states that a calculated approach is necessary until mutual respect and equality are achieved. An earlier version of this article was published in *Having Children: Philosophical and Legal Reflections on Parenthood* (New York: Oxford University Press, 1979).

51. Hoffnung, Michele. "Motherhood: Contemporary Conflict for Women" (1984) in Jo Freeman, ed. *Women: A Feminist Perspective*. 4th ed. Palo Alto, Calif.: Mayfield, 1989, pp. 124–138.

    Hoffnung sees motherhood's limiting effect on women's participation in the public sector as a primary concern to feminist actions for social change. Her solution, like that of Ruddick (80, 81), is that the value of mothering be reconsidered and public priorities be reorganized so that both men and women participate in mothering. Hoffnung notes two sets of expectations for women which are in conflict: successful individual accomplishment and responsibility for family life. She goes on to debunk four aspects of the "Motherhood Mystique: " ultimate fulfillment as a woman through mothering; the complementarity of childcare, home care, and husband care; "good enough" mothering; and finally, the benefits to both children and mothers of exclusive mothering. This article includes a good synopsis of many contemporary studies on mothering, most of which are cited in this bibliography. Hoffnung concludes that young women should prepare ahead for combining work and family by careful choice of careers and mates.

52. Holland, Barbara. *Mother's Day: Or, The View From in Here*. Garden City, N.Y.: Doubleday, 1980.

    This is an autobiographical account of a former advertising employee turned mother and housewife. Although somewhat in the tradition of Erma Bombeck, Holland's story is more melancholic and reflective. For many feminists the humor may be impossible to find, as Holland bemoans nearly every detail of her daily life but never questions the nature of her role or her decision to take it on. Her writing is quietly powerful and will give an authentic look at this lifestyle.

53. *Hypatia*. Special Issue: Motherhood and Sexuality. 1: 2 (Fall 1986).

    This issue of *Hypatia*, which was edited by Ann Ferguson (see 37, 38), includes a number of academic essays, two of which have been separately annotated, see Ferguson (234) and Donchin

(337). Janice Raymond's "Female Friendship: Contra Chodorow and Dinnerstein" critiques these two theorists for giving scant attention to women's relations to each other; Reyes Lazaro's "Feminism and Motherhood: O'Brien vs. Beauvoir" argues that both O'Brien's celebratory analysis and de Beauvoir's critical one of motherhood fail due to biologism and a lack of historical perspective while Janet Farrel-Smith's "Possessive Power" utilizes de Beauvoir's account of maternity. Other essays are concerned with feminist sexuality in general and the theories of Foucault and Lacan.

54. Johnson, Miriam H. *Strong Mothers, Weak Wives: The Search for Gender Equality*. Berkeley: University of California Press, 1988.

Johnson states that she is addressing feminists and is concerned with how gender inequality is reproduced and how it might be changed. Although the male dominated context of women's childbearing and rearing creates inequality, Johnson points out that it is the inequalities of marriage which subordinate women, not their role as mothers. She believes that women's mothering produces solidarity while her role as a wife separates her from other women. She sees the roots of the patriarchal social order in which mothers become wives as stemming from male dominance, which in turn comes from men's roles as fathers and from male peer groups. This is a variation on the theories of Dinnerstein (27) and Chodorow (19) which blame men's dominance on the mothering of women. Johnson writes from a psychoanalytical perspective and connects the fact of women's childbearing to orientational differences between women and men, such as women's greater relational capacity (see Gilligan, 324). But these differences do not justify women's confinement to domesticity or lesser jobs; Johnson says that it is not gender difference itself but what we do with it which creates inequality. Unlike Chodorow and Dinnerstein, Johnson believes that shared parenting will reinforce male dominance unless marriages first become truly equal. *Strong Mothers* includes an extensive, up to date bibliography.

55. Kitzinger, Shelia. *Women as Mothers: How They See Themselves In Different Cultures*. New York: Random House, 1979.

    The author is a social anthropologist and from this viewpoint she examines mothering from a cross-cultural and cross-class perspective. She has a definite bias toward being a mother and a good part of this book is spent on pregnancy, childbirth and caring for infants. She sees the family and mothers' roles in it as a basis for change in society, particularly through shared parenting. Although Kitzenger sees the role of motherhood positively and seems slightly in favor of this being the best choice for women, not just one of many choices, she offers some interesting insights to the experience of motherhood, such as in communal situations including Communist China, the kibbutz, present day communes and the nineteenth-century Oneida Community.

56. Kohler, Bertram J., and Henry U. Grunebaum. *Mothers, Grandmothers, and Daughters: Personality and Childcare in Three-Generation Families*. New York: John Wiley, 1981.

    This is a study of four Italian-American families which looks at the relationship between three generations of women: mothers, daughters and grandmothers. It was done from a social science perspective as informed by psychoanalysis and is based on lengthy interviews over six years. The authors, both men, state that the results of this study might have been different had it been conducted by women. The first and last chapters look at intergenerational relations and continuities. Among the conclusions which the authors reach is that life-long interdependence or lack of separateness between women is the norm. This closeness often accelerates at the time of childbearing. The authors also found that grown adult daughters often want a closer relationship with their mothers just at the point when the mother is finally willing to separate due to her own needs as she enters old age. The intervening chapters look closely at each of the families and offer insights into the individual relations. See Fischer (105), Hayes (197) and Price (216) for other generational studies.

57. Kornfein, Madeleine, Thomas Weisner and Joan Martin. "Women into Mothers: Experimental Family Life-Styles" in Jane Roberts Chapman and Margaret Gates, eds. *Women into Wives: The Legal and Economic Impact of Marriage*. London and Beverly Hills: Sage Publications, 1977, pp. 259–291.

As a woman becomes a mother she must deal with a variety of concerns including basic necessities for survival, new social networks, additional household tasks coupled with a need for time to bond with her infant, the responsibility for nurturance of the child, changes in her relationship with her partner if she is not single and often the need to express herself as an individual and productive being. Some women can meet these needs within a conventional family setting, others are choosing alternatives. These include single mothering, either by choice or circumstance, social contracts whereby a couple lives together by contractual agreement and collective living. The authors compare women in these groups to each other and to legally married women in order to see how the needs defined above are being met. As the study is longitudinal, the authors do not offer any specific conclusions but many interesting insights are included such as the idea that freedom is always relative: the mother in the collective has more free time but must always consider the needs of many others; the single mother has great autonomy but cannot function spontaneously as she must always be arranging for childcare. See 162 for another entry by Kornfein and Weisner.

58. Lazarre, Jane. *The Mother Knot*. (1976). Boston: McGraw-Hill, 1986.

The Mother Knot offers perceptive insights into the reality of motherhood with a personal account of one woman's experience and her attempt to overturn the myths surrounding the actual experience. Yet, despite her ability with lyrical and evocatively descriptive prose, Lazarre has a tendency to whine. She writes from the white middle-class perspective of the "motherwife" and from within an interracial marriage which does not seem to be problematic, yet she complains incessantly about the isolation of mothering while doing nothing to alleviate the situation and seemingly being unaware of the choices she might have as compared to many women.

Sara Ruddick's new introduction to *The Mother Knot* is a good starting point for readers, as well as a useful afterthought when one has finished this difficult book. Ruddick gives an overview of mothering in today's society as she sees it, admitting her bias but withholding judgment. See Rossiter (77) and Ruddick's essay in Dourick's, *Why Children?* (28) for similar experiences to that of Lazarre.

59. Levy, Marion J. *Our Mother-Tempers*. Berkeley: University of California Press, 1989.

Levy addresses the developmental effects of the predominant role of mothers in childrearing, including the preponderance of male-dominated societies. He gives credit to Chodorow and Dinnerstein and discusses their work at length but says his interest is in the effects of mothering on the basic structure of all societies. Levy states that mothers teach sons their masculinity as well as giving them the idea that fathers offer the more important influences on a child's life, although Levy states that both the mothers and the children who believe this to be true are wrong. Like many feminist theorists, he is concerned with the reproduction of male domination.

60. Lorber, Judith, Rose Coser and Alice Rossi. "On *The Reproduction of Mothering*: A Methodological Debate." *Signs* 6: 3 (Spring 1981): 482–514.

This is a collection of three responses by Lorber, Coser and Rossi to *The Reproduction of Mothering* (19) with a reply from Chodorow. Lorber suggests that Chodorow's earlier pieces (see 100, 300) are more a contribution to the sociology of gender than *The Reproduction of Mothering*. This book, according to Lorber, uses only clinical case histories to support the author's theories and has an emphasis on psychoanalysis to the exclusion of social structures. Lorber believes that to change men and women we need to change the social structure which produces current parenting arrangements. Coser basically agrees with Chodorow's thesis and extends it into a more structural analysis while Rossi agrees with Lorber that Chodorow's thesis is too embedded in psychodynamic terms, yet she applauds Chodorow's core insight into female gender development. Chodorow defends herself as defining mothering in terms of a social structure.

61. Maglin, Nan Bauer, and Nancy Schneidewind, eds. *Women and Stepfamilies. Voices of Anger and Love*. Philadelphia: Temple University, 1989.

There are 35, 000, 000 stepparents in America with 1, 300 new stepfamilies forming everyday. Although there is a great deal of current literature on stepfamilies, including a bibliography by Ellen J. Gruber, *Stepfamilies: A Guide to the Sources and Resources* (Garland, 1986) this is the first book written from a feminist perspective and the woman's point of view. The editors explain the use of the term "stepfamily" over "blended" because the latter assumes integration and hides the differences which should be acknowledged and accepted. These women's accounts raise questions about mothering: who is a mother and what constitutes a family? They also point out that feminist insight is often not a match for the power of emotional experience. Many of the authors bring up the image of the "good mother" versus the "wicked stepmother" mythology. Part I consists of perspectives from ten stepmothers, four mothers, nine stepdaughters and two stepgrandmothers which take the form of interviews, stories, poems and first person narratives. Part II, "Stepping Out," is written by women who have removed themselves, at least temporarily, from their families and Part III, "Transforming," offers accounts of dealing with specific problems in stepfamilies. According to Maglin and Schneidewind, "women in stepfamilies have the potential for transforming both the women's' role as mother and the family itself."

62. Maraini, Dacia. "On *Of Woman Born*." Translated by Mary Jane Ciccarello. *Signs* 4: 4 (Summer 1979): 687–694.

A favorable review of Rich's book (76), written from Italy, which discusses issues of feminine writing, motherhood, mother-daughter relationships and the women's movement in Italy.

63. Matthews, Sanford J., and Maryann Bucknum Brinley. *Through the Motherhood Maze.* Garden City, N.Y.: Doubleday, 1982.

    The two authors, one a mother and writer, the other a male pediatrician, are concerned with how some women can lose themselves in the mothering role to such an extent that this takes over their whole lives. They see this phenomenon as cheating both the mother and her child of experiencing the full potential of the mother's life. Matthews also notes that a large number of male doctors (obstetricians, pediatricians) are contemptuous of women's ability to mother well, an attitude which of course has negative consequences for women. The "solution" Brinley and Matthews suggest for women to retain their identity in the process of mothering is to develop their own strengths and care about themselves, even before their children. They analyze pregnancy, the birth experience and the transition to motherhood in case histories of seven mothers (see Bergum 7, Eakins 29 and Fischer 105 for other works on this transition). Although not particularly a feminist book, it is certainly pro-women and supportive of their rights as individuals.

64. McBride, Angela Barron. *The Growth and Development of Mothers.* New York: Harper & Row, 1973.

    This book offers an early look at the motherhood mystique, the reasons women choose to have children and how they can move beyond this way of thinking. Like many of the books which predate Rich's *Of Women Born* (76), including Peck and Senderowitz (72), Bernard (8) and Radl (75), McBride's work shows an awareness of the primary assumptions concerning motherhood: a baby is woman's ultimate achievement and women are best suited for the raising of children. She is also writing from the era when feminism was either ignoring or denigrating motherhood as being a cop-out, which makes these early works interesting when doing a study of the changes and attitudes toward mothering which have taken place over the past two decades. McBride is very supportive of women's abilities to raise children, which she points out are often dismissed by proponents of the motherhood mystique who often criticize women's actual mothering.

65. McCabe, Jane. Review of *Of Woman Born: Motherhood as Experience and Institution* (76). *Frontiers: A Journal of Women Studies* 3: 2 (Summer 1978): 77–78.

McCabe defends Rich as not being against motherhood or having children but rather as distinguishing between the socially accepted ideology and the realistic experience of mothering. She acknowledges that Rich incorporates both personal and public life as part of her feminist politics. It is a well-written and succinct review.

66. Minturn, Leigh, and William L. Lambert. *Mothers of Six Cultures: Antecedents of Child Rearing*. New York: Wiley, 1964.

Minturn and Lambert point out that the uniqueness of Western mothers' practice of exclusive child-rearing results, in many cases, in irritability and emotional instability for the mother, rather than warmth toward the children (see Boulton, 11 for similar findings). Although dated, this book offers an interesting cross-cultural perspective from an early feminist viewpoint. The cultures examined include Africa, Mexico, Japan, India, the Philippines and the United States.

67. Mullan, Bob. *Are Mothers Really Necessary?* New York: Weidenfeld & Nicolson, 1988.

Mullan attempts to reconcile the British psychiatrist John Bowlby's views (see Mullan's bibliography for numerous references to Bowlby's works) on mothering, as done by mothers, as necessary for the optimum development of the child with two recent feminist ideologies: that women can and should work outside the home and, that mothers are not responsible for all of society's problems. Mullan states "It is my contention that both Bowlby and the more modern feminist writers like Rich, Dinnerstein, Arcana et al., offer genuinely useful guidelines" (p. 142). Yet, there is something that makes one uneasy with this book such as when Mullan says that motherhood should be freed from its institutionalized shackles and be seen as the most important work anyone can do notwithstanding that men are not psychologically able to mother, at least at this time. Since

Bowlby's views on mothering are so controversial, this book is an interesting exercise in male apologetic writing.

68. Oakley, Ann. *Women Confined: Towards a Sociology of Childbirth.* (1979). New York: Schocken Books, 1980.

Oakley's analysis deals with the way motherhood is part of a socially constructed femininity within Western culture. Her thesis is that a woman's passage into motherhood within the capitalist patriarchy is a process of demobilization: a loss of control, alienation and dependency. She believes that this is the reality of the experience of motherhood, as opposed to the image. This idea is, of course, similar to those of Rich (76), Lewis (118) and Westkott (131). See Oakley's other work (69).

69. Oakley, Ann. *Becoming a Mother.* (1979). New York: Schocken Books, 1980.

Based on interviews with 66 women expecting their first babies, *Becoming a Mother* is essentially a guide book for childbirth and new mothers written from a refreshingly feminist perspective. Oakley is a feminist academic sociologist and mother who states that her research was done in the new feminist method which incorporated her own personal experiences with those of the women she interviewed. Although this book falls more into the category of "how-to" books, its feminist perspective makes it one of the few of its genre. See Oakley's other work (68).

70. O'Donnell, Lydia. *The Unheralded Majority: Contemporary Women as Mothers.* Lexington, Mass.: Lexington Books, 1985.

This is a study of middle-class mothers who have a degree of choice in their lives but are nevertheless limited by the constraints of family. O'Donnell is a feminist who believed, if given the choice, women would choose interesting, well-paid jobs over full-time mothering. However, O'Donnell became a mother herself and thereby part of a community of mothers wherein she met mothers who felt otherwise. (See Lazarre, 58 and Ruddick's essay in Dourick's *Why Children?*, 28 for similar accounts.) The majority of these mothers felt that their first responsibility was to their families. O'Donnell asks whether we will see these women as victims of male supremacy and reactionaries to the women's movement or, as O'Donnell herself does, as a pivotal generation incorporating the strengths of the women's movement while recognizing its weaknesses. O'Donnell neglects to point out that not everyone has a choice of full-time mothering, nor does she investigate the connection of full-time mothering to the perpetuation of patriarchy (see Heffner, 49 for the same bias). O'Donnell's thesis on this subject is in the Gutman Education division of the Harvard Archives.

71. Paskowicz, Patricia. *Absentee Mothers*. New York: Universe Books, 1982.

The author concludes that absentee mothers are not harming their children, but rather any problems the children may encounter are due to the traumas of the divorce and are comparable to those problems of children remaining with their mothers. According to one table of three studies which Paskowicz cites, children of absentee mothers may actually be less affected by divorce. The author relinquished custody of her three children because she felt that she couldn't survive in her role of traditional wife and mother. She used a questionnaire which resulted in a sample of 100 women from across the U.S., primarily white, middle and working-class and interspersed her findings with autobiographical material. She found that there is much anger and hostility toward absentee mothers who are often portrayed as selfish and sexually promiscuous. Many absentee mothers were daughters who had been abandoned by their own mothers. Others included women married to rigid husbands who had unplanned children. Unfortunately, it seems that many of the women suffered both from their own guilt as well as that imposed upon them by society and consequently were often as unhappy as they had been in their previous lives. See Edwards (30) and Greif (46) for other studies on non-custodial mothers.

72. Peck, Ellen, and Judith Senderowitz, eds. *Pronatalism. The Myth of Mom & Apple Pie*. New York: Thomas Crowell, 1974.

Pronatalism is defined here as any attitude or policy that encourages reproduction and celebrates parenthood. This collection of 24 essays looks at the pressures to bear children that existed in the early 1970s within North American society as evidenced in women's magazine fiction, television, high school courses and sociology textbooks. Next, the issue of motherhood is addressed, particularly the motivations toward wanting children. Robert Gould, in his essay "The Wrong Reasons to have Children," gives twelve misconceptions including having a baby to save a marriage and because parents want grandchildren. The last nine essays are concerned with voluntary childlessness, how this trend has come about and why some couples are choosing to be childfree. In "A Vote Against Motherhood" Gael Greene states that she and her husband chose not to have children because they enjoy their time together, are both interested in their work and feel (rightly so) that a child would interfere with these areas. The consensus of these authors is that parenthood is not inevitable nor is it appropriate for all people, yet there are serious biases against those who choose to be child free and strong social forces producing a universal ideal of parenthood.

73. Polatnic, M. Rivka. "Why Men Don't Rear Children: A Power Analysis" (1973) in Joyce Trebilcot, ed. *Mothering: Essays in Feminist Theory*. Totowa, N.J.: Rowman & Allanheld, 1984, pp. 21–40.

    Polatnic, who is only concerned with current trends in society, sees the social policy of women caring for children as supportive of male dominance both within society and the family. She says that men do not want to take care of children because of the lack of pay, status and power. We can certainly see the truth in this by the lack of men at home, in day care and in the elementary school system. The benefit is obvious for men: they have the services of wives in running their household and in mothers in rearing their children. This article is an excerpt from a paper originally published in the *Berkeley Journal of Sociology* 18 (1973–74): 45–86.

74. Price, Jane. *Motherhood: What It Does To Your Mind*. London: Pandora Press, 1988.

Written by a feminist psychiatrist, this book looks at how modern society and culture treat the role of mothering and the work of mothers in an unrealistic and trivial fashion. Price bases her theories on observations with her patients as well as her own experience as a mother. She begins by looking at the connection between unresolved conflicts in a mother's own childhood and the way in which she interacts with her children (see Alice Miller, 291–293). This leads to finding an image of a "true" as opposed to "perfect" mother who does not suffer from a false self but is able to treat her child with honesty and respect. She feels that only women and men who share both childrearing and outside work pressures are able to enjoy a true sense of communication. In contrast to Kohler and Grunebaum (56), Price notes that the transition from mother/daughter to mother/daughter/grandmother is often a time when past hostilities are put to rest and a deeper closeness is achieved. In relation to single mothers, Price points out that there are many women living as single mothers within marriages and that once women get over the emotional and financial repercussions of divorce, many report being happier and more self-assured.

75. Radl, Shirley L. *Mother's Day is Over*. New York: Charterhouse, 1973.

This is an early book written by a mother, from interviews with 200 women of various class and educational backgrounds, about the difficulties of mothering. She examines the contradiction of loving her children while disliking the actual experience of motherhood. She recognizes a loss of identity and self-worth as due to full-time mothering yet still believes that Dr. Spock is correct in saying that mothers raising children full time is best for the children. A later book by Radl, *How to Be a Mother—And a Person Too* (1989), was written mainly as a self-help book for mothers struggling with their feelings about themselves and their children.

76. Rich, Adrienne. *Of Woman Born: Motherhood as Experience and Institution*. (1976). Tenth Anniversary Edition. New York: W.W. Norton & Company, 1986.

When first published, this book raised a good deal of critical anger as it was incorrectly perceived as being against the family and mothering; but it has also been hailed as one of the most important books of feminist analysis. See Bart (5), Eisenstein (32), Haaken (47), Hirsch (114), Lewis (118), Maraini (62) and McCabe (65) for reviews of this work. The central core of Rich's argument is her distinction between the experience (female) and the institution (male) of motherhood. These ideas were set out two years earlier by Bernard in *The Future of Motherhood* (8). This is not an attack on mothering per se but on how mothering functions within the patriarchy. Rather than eliminating childbirth, as advocated by Firestone (305), Rich wants to alter the conditions of motherhood. She sees its institutions (economic dependence of marriage, laws regulating contraception and abortion, male doctors controlling childbirth, the concept of illegitimacy) as negative for women but the experience as positive. She looks at mothering both cross-culturally and historically. This remains one of the major feminist studies on mothering. Rich's papers are held at the Schlesinger library.

77. Rossiter, Amy. *From Private to Public: A Feminist Exploration of Early Mothering*. Toronto: The Women's Press, 1988.

    Like Lazarre (58) and O'Donnell (70), Rossiter looks at the contradictions of early mothering from her own experience as well as those of three other women. She analyzes, from a feminist perspective, the social conditions which make mothering both "joyous and oppressive."

78. Rubin, Lillian B. *Women of a Certain Age: The Midlife Search for Self*. New York: Harper & Row, 1979.

    Rubin looks at mothers in the "empty nest syndrome" when children are gone and these women must confront the future. She interviews 160 women between the ages of 35 and 54 from a cross-section of America with one half working outside of the home, mostly in pink collar jobs, a few committed volunteers, a few having returned to school and over one half who call themselves homemakers and want to remain so. She looks at the common experiences of women who take marriage and motherhood as their primary life task. She finds that most are relieved when the children are gone and suffer depression, not at the loss of the children, but at the fact that they do not have any other interest with which to fulfill themselves. Rubin herself underwent the experience noted by Betty Friedan in *The Feminine Mystique* of finding herself in 1962 with a husband and child she loved but without enough meaningful work to fill up her life.

79. Rubin, Nancy. *The Mother Mirror: How a Generation of Women is Changing Motherhood in America*. New York: Putnam, 1984.

Unlike Fabe and Wikler (35) and McKaughan (209), Rubin feels that it is no longer necessary for women to agonize over the choice of work versus motherhood for a variety of reasons: economic necessity, the de-mystification and de-valuing of motherhood and the knowledge that women, like men, are usually happiest when performing several roles, including work and nurturance. The form of motherhood which Rubin suggests is based on both the mother's and the child's needs with the woman preparing herself for motherhood by becoming economically independent, realizing that motherhood is transitory, prioritizing long-term life goals, preparing for separation from her child and avoiding feelings of guilt. This is similar to the suggestions of Matthews and Brinley (63).

80. Ruddick, Sara. "Maternal Thinking" (1980) in Joyce Trebilcot, ed. *Mothering: Essays in Feminist Theory*. Totowa, N.J.: Rowman & Allanheld, 1984, pp. 213–230.

Ruddick points out that all aspects of women's thought, be it related to maternal or world matters, will be influenced by powerlessness since thought arises out of social practice. She sees mothers as engaging in a discipline which includes establishing certain criteria. The mother's interests include preserving the child, fostering its growth and shaping it into acceptability—the same interests which characterize much human activity. Maternal thinking is a unity of reflection, judgment and emotion. This is a fascinating essay which celebrates the responsibilities of mothering and bears reading by all feminist thinkers and mothers alike. Ruddick concludes that bringing men into parenting (as per the advice of Dinnerstein, 27 and Chodorow, 19) is not necessarily the solution but rather, we should work to bring maternal thought into the public realm so that everyone begins to mother (see Hoffnung, 51). A longer version of this essay was published in *Feminist Studies* 6: 2 (Summer 1980) and this version is also published in Barrie Thorne's *Rethinking the Family* (281). See Ruddick's other works generally on mothering (28) and on this particular aspect (81, 89).

81. Ruddick, Sara. *Maternal Thinking: Toward A Politics of Peace.* Boston: Beacon, 1989.

Ruddick begins this book by saying that although she speaks as a mother, what she has to say reflects her experience as a daughter. She enlarges on the ideas first presented in her article, "Preservation Love and Military Destruction: Some Reflections on Mothering and Peace" (1982) which was published in Trebilcot's collection of essays (80). Ruddick feels that mothers do not necessarily share virtues pertaining to mothering but rather, share a discourse concerning the strengths needed for their ongoing commitment to protect and nurture. Ruddick offers the concept of feminist maternal peace politics which starts by repudiating the myth that mothers are peace-makers without power since almost everywhere that men fight, they are supported by their mothers. Maternal abilities of men and women may contribute to peace but maternal practice must first be transformed into the work of peace. The practice of mothering gives rise to ways of thinking and doing that are useful to peace politics—the idea that people who mother well are committed to non-violent action, to truth and to love. This complex work, which needs a close reading to fully understand its thesis, offers an actual course for change. See Ruddick's other earlier essay on this subject, published in *Women's Studies Quarterly* (89).

82. Russo, Nancy F. "The Motherhood Mandate." *Journal of Social Issues* 32: 3 (1976): 143–153.

Russo looks at the social and cultural forces which propel women into motherhood with a review of current literature. She suggests that this mandate provides resistance to change and that sex-typed behavior can only be altered by attacking the mandate while providing adequate childcare for existing families.

83. Snitow, Ann. "Thinking About *The Mermaid and the Minotaur*." *Feminist Studies* 4: 2 (June 1978): 192–198.

Snitow first offers a succinct summary of Dinnerstein's (27) often difficult, and as Snitow states, circular, arguments. She points out that Dinnerstein's ideas are both complex and theoretical and that Dinnerstein comes close to equating the female monopoly of childcare with the cause of misogyny. Yet, Snitow feels that Dinnerstein "is, very simply, one of the great humanists we have writing now." Snitow sees motherhood in a condition of crisis and Dinnerstein as diagnosing the symptoms and offering a solution of dual parenting.

84. Spencer, Anita. *Mothers Are People Too: A Contemporary Analysis of Motherhood.* Ramsey, N.J.: Paulist Press, 1984.

Based on psychological literature and on her own experiences as a counselor, especially for displaced homemakers, Spencer writes a broad, easily accessible analysis of the problems and contemporary contradictions of motherhood. Discussing such topics as the Madonna and Child archetype of the "good mother" and Hans Sebald's concept of "Momism," she writes in a supportive tone, indirectly appealing to mothers who, like herself, feel in conflict and would like to understand the nature of their mothering. Interesting sections on the future of mothering and on the relationship between mothering and religious fundamentalism appear at the end of the book.

85. Tiffany, Sharon W. *Women, Work, and Motherhood: The Power of Female Sexuality in the Work Place.* Englewood Cliffs, N.J.: Prentice-Hall, 1982.

Written from a feminist-anthropological perspective, Tiffany examines childbearing and work by women, particularly in third world countries. She focuses on universalities in women's lives, such as male dominance, as well as diversities in the female experience. She looks at women's roles as farmers, herders, gardeners and mothers and points out the irony that as western women turn to more natural methods of birth control, delivery and feeding of infants, third world women are being encouraged to use IUD's, hospital births and infant formulas.

86. Trebilcot, Joyce, ed. *Mothering: Essays in Feminist Theory.* Totowa, N.J.: Rowman & Allanheld, 1984.

    This is a collection of 18 essays written between 1972 and 1982, some published here for the first time, which are divided into four sections: "Who is to look after the children?," "Mothering and the explanation of patriarchy," "Concepts of mothering" and "Pronatalism and resistance." Trebilcot notes in her introduction that the essays address the meanings of mothering within patriarchy as well as the possibilities of feminist mothering outside of it. All 18 authors and the editor describe themselves as feminists in a section written by the contributors. Most of the essays have been annotated separately within this bibliography (see 1, 5, 31, 37, 50, 73, 80, 250, 296, 308, 309, 310, 312).

87. Wearing, Betsy. *The Ideology of Motherhood: A Study of Sydney Suburban Mothers.* Boston: Allen & Unwin, 1984.

    This work consists of interviews with 150 mothers that reflect a set of ideas and beliefs surrounding mothering. The main one Wearing uncovers is the belief that it is the natural and the inevitable responsibility of biological mothers to raise their children. This eliminates the idea of working mothers and day care. Wearing believes this ideology places severe limitations on the lives of women, even though they do derive a certain satisfaction from being mothers. Wearing investigates just whose interests are served by this ideology and comes to the conclusion, of course, that it is the patriarchy. She looks at various types of mothers: working and middle-class, feminist, employed and single.

88. Whitbeck, Carolyn. "The Maternal Instinct" (1974) in Joyce Trebilcot, ed. *Mothering: Essays in Feminist Theory.* Totowa, N.J.: Rowman & Allanheld, 1984, pp. 185–198.

Written from a philosophical viewpoint, Whitbeck points out the male bias in philosophy which, like so many disciplines, has given little thought to traits or dispositions particularly significant in women. Whitbeck argues that the quality of maternal attachment is determined by the woman's actual experience of pregnancy and childbirth. Although she does not specifically mention adoption, the quality of the prospective adoptive mother's experience in the adoption process certainly seems relevant to subsequent attachment. Whitbeck concludes that although parental *attachment* or affection is influenced cross-culturally by biological factors this does not necessarily constitute a maternal *instinct.* An afterword in 1982 follows the article in the form of a letter to her adolescent daughter that encompasses a review of feminist literature on mothering written over the past decade. This article was first published in *The Philosophical Forum* 6: 2–3 (Winter-Spring, 1974–1975).

89. *Women's Studies Quarterly.* Special Issue: Teaching About Mothering. 11: 4 (Winter 1983).

This complete issue, dedicated to mothering, consists of a short, annotated bibliography on mothering and mother-daughter relationships by Marianne Hirsch, (see 114 for a review essay on mothers and daughters by Hirsch), descriptions of various courses on mothering, including one taught by Trebilcot (see 86 for Trebilcot's book), reviews of books, prose pieces, a short story, essays on mothers and daughters in fiction, and Chicana myths of motherhood. Also included is "Thinking about Mothering—and Putting Maternal Thinking to Use" by Sara Ruddick (see her other works on this subject, 80, 81). Two additional essays have been annotated separately: one on lesbian motherhood by Evelyn Beck (230) and a critique of Rich, Chodorow and Dinnerstein by Janice Haaken (47).

II.

Mothers and Daughters: Together and Apart

"The loss of the daughter to the mother, the mother to the daughter, is the essential female tragedy" according to Adrienne Rich in *Of Woman Born* (76), p. 237.

The daughter to mother transition is both additive and sequential: we keep our role as daughters at the same time as we become mothers. In recent years this transition, particularly through adolescence, has become more difficult. Rich traces the reasons for this to contemporary patriarchy, which she argues keeps women apart, by keeping them in conflict and competition.

Luce Irigaray (115) believes patriarchy actually requires the separation of the mother and daughter to exist while Rich attempts to heal the rift. The relationship of mothers and daughters to patriarchy must continue to be investigated. Many of the authors cited below have incorporated this question in their studies.

When studying mothers and their daughters, one must be aware of the specific cultural differences which affect the relationship. For example, black women are more likely to be single mothers.[1] According to Gloria Joseph in *Common Differences* (257), black women are socialized by their mothers and their grandmothers to be strong and independent because they know that the effects of poverty and racism will often result in these daughters becoming the heads of households. Carol Stack (260) found in her study of a black community that childrearing was a totally different experience than for members of the white community, with much more kin interaction.

Joseph also found that black daughters generally have a high regard for their mothers. This is in contrast to the white daughters in

Judith Arcana's interviews, who fear being like their mothers. The core of role representation for these daughters is supposedly found in their mothers yet 63% say they consciously try not to be like their mothers (*Our Mothers' Daughters* 92, p. 9).

In searching for a reason to explain white daughters' attitudes, Jill Lewis (118) says that this fear is not due to lack of respect but to a fear of the conditions of motherhood which, in the white family, seem to reproduce patriarchy. This matrophobia, this fear of becoming like one's own mother is rooted in patriarchy; it comes from our rage at the powerlessness of our mothers.

Social class is another variable in mother-daughter relations. Working-class mothers see their primary role as wife and mother, even if they hold a job whereas middle-class women perceive their careers and mothering as equally important parts of their lives. According to Edith Neisser (120), many working-class daughters see their working mother as the authority figure while daughters of all races and classes are more likely to be influenced by their mother's occupational status than by their father's (Pearson, 123).

What are some of the positive aspects of this relationship as it exists today? In her study of mothers and their adult daughters, Lucy Fischer (105) found that mothers and daughters who maintained peerlike relations had a high level of involvement in each other's lives. Numerous other studies (see Hoffman 199, Baruch 93 and Shreve 223) have pointed out that girls who have positive role models in their working mothers tend to be high achievers and more successful in their lives. Along with the benefit of a positive role model, many daughters of working mothers have gained from their androgynous upbringings by avoiding falling into traditional patterns (see Lynn 119, Hansen and Chernovetz 196 and Hoffman 198).

Evelyn Bassoff's (94) study of mothers and adolescent daughters offers an interesting hypothesis that the developmental tasks of each are interrelated, i.e., the daughter's need to differentiate complements the mother's own separation from her daughter. Marianne Walters (98) echoes this with the idea that the daughter's rebellion is a plea for the mother to show her own strength. If mothers and daughters can begin to see these connections, they could possibly avoid many of the conflicts inherent in this relationship.

However, there are many contradictions in mother/daughter relations: remaining close while going separate ways, becoming peers while remaining parent and child. Another contradiction is that the child needs the mother's capacities as a nurturer but if the mother sacrifices her independence for her daughter, the daughter has no basis for identification. As Jessica Benjamin has noted, the recognition the child seeks can only be given by a mother who has a separate identity (*The Bonds of Love* 316, p. 24).

Some mothers and daughters don't have a strong sense of intimacy and attachment for any number of reasons: the mother's and/or daughter's personality, lack of financial or educational resources and perhaps most importantly, the quality and amount of time spent together. According to Alice Miller (291–293), the success of the mother largely depends on the quality of mothering she herself has received. But even if a mother has not been well-mothered herself, this pattern can change if she is able to accept her losses and not attempt to heal them through her child.

It is important to look at the mother-daughter relationship in the context of a society which devalues this bond and understand that we are not acting freely when we relate to each other. A recurring theme in the work of Arcana (92) and Paula Caplan (96) is the search by both the mother and daughter for more complete mothering. This can only come when we accept our mothers and our daughters for who they are. When the daughter becomes a mother there is often a chance for a new beginning, for another source of identification between these two women.

Although many problems for mothers and daughters have been noted here and in the books cited below, there is evidence of change in the relations between mothers and daughters as seen in the letters edited by Karen Payne (122) and in another recent book, *Conversations with Mothers and Daughters*, by Celia Dodd (London: Macdonald Optima, 1990). As strong, feminist mothers begin to raise their daughters there is less and less the injurious double message of independence/femininity sent by mothers to their daughters.

It is important for mothers and daughters to work at their relationships because for society to change, for patriarchy to end, there must be strong mothers and daughters. "The quality of the mother's life—however embattled and unprotected—is her primary bequest to her daughter . . . " (Rich, p. 247).

Notes

1. U.S. Department of Commerce. 1986. Current Population Reports, Series P-20, #411.

BIBLIOGRAPHY—
MOTHERS AND DAUGHTERS

90. Abramson, Jane B. *Mothermania: A Psychological Study of Mother—Daughter Conflict*. Lexington, Mass.: Lexington Books, 1987.

This is a study of the psychological adaptations of 39 mothers over 60 years old to the deaths of their own mothers, conducted through various psychological tests. It focuses on the question of whether the experience of being a mother offers the possibility of overcoming early developmental deficiencies. The conclusions suggest that mothering can offer some means of growth and change but not when it is the exclusive role in a woman's life. Abramson found through her study of older mothers that their ability to use the experience of mothering for their own personal development (much less the development of their daughters) depended on the kind of mothering that they had received. Abramson used TAT (picture cards) to measure separation-individuation and found that women who have separated successfully from their mothers function better than women who have not.

91. (Arcana) Pildes, Judith. "Mothers and Daughters: Understanding the Roles." *Frontiers: A Journal of Women Studies* 3: 2 (1978): 1–11.

Pildes, who also writes under the name of Arcana, basically gives a condensed version of her book, *Our Mothers' Daughters*

(92). This is a good introduction to Arcana's interviews with 120 daughters that are presented more thoroughly in her later work.

92. Arcana, Judith. *Our Mothers' Daughters*. Berkeley: Shameless Hussy Press, 1979.

Even though a decade old, *Our Mothers' Daughters* is still applicable to relations today between mothers and daughters. It is based on 120 sensitive interviews conducted with women between the ages of 14 and 68. Arcana intersperses her synopsis of the data and her views on mothers and daughters with quotes from the interviews which makes this book flow well. She includes a good annotated bibliography and the questions she used in her interviews. She has written the book to help "confront the reality of our mothers, as the women they are, and as they live in us." She points out that the core of role representation for daughters is in their mothers, yet over 60% of the women interviewed said they had tried *not* to model themselves on their mothers. A recurring theme in the book is the search, both by mothers and daughters, for more complete mothering. Arcana believes our present society so systematically devalues women that mothers and daughters don't look to each other for support, Rich's (76) "essential female tragedy." This also relates to Dinnerstein's (27) thesis that women's lack of self-esteem contributes to male dominance. In Arcana's study one-half of the women preferred their fathers over their mothers although only about one-fourth of these fathers took an active role in raising their children. This is a book that can be recommended to any mother or daughter to read as she will inevitably find something of herself within it. See Hirsch (114) for a critique of Arcana's work.

93. Baruch, Grace K. "Girls Who Perceive Themselves as Competent: Some Antecedents and Correlates." *Psychology of Women Quarterly* 1: 1 (Fall 1976): 38–49.

This is a study of 79 fifth graders and 49 tenth graders and their mothers on self-perceptions of competence. The results showed girls who had high self-perceptions as having mothers whose own self-perceptions were high and who placed more value on traits such as independence, assertiveness and achievement. Working papers by Baruch on mothers and daughters are at the Schlesinger Library and the Center for Research on Women at Wellesley College. See Baruch's other articles (180, 297, 314).

94. Bassoff, Evelyn. *Mothers and Daughters: Loving and Letting Go.* New York: New American Library, 1988.

This book looks at adolescent daughters from the viewpoint of the mother who, by separating from her daughter, will become more fulfilled in her own life and hence, a more loving mother. Bassoff shows conflicting aspects of mothering for both the mother and the daughter from a positive point of view and believes that the developmental tasks of the middle-aged mother and adolescent daughter are interrelated. The author has used psychological literature and her experience as a psychotherapist, as well as myths and fairy-tales in her study. She is also the mother of an adolescent daughter. This book contains chapters on single mothers, adoptive mothers and stepmothers. Bassoff states that one of the best things single mothers can do for their daughters is to empower them: to help them feel in control and to be effective. A later article by Bassoff, "Mothering Adolescent Daughters: A Psychodynamic Perspective," has been published in the *Journal of Counseling and Development* 9 (1987): 471–475.

95. Cahill, Susan, Abbott, et al., eds. *Mothers: Memories, Dreams, and Reflections by Literary Daughters.* New York: New American Library, 1988.

This is an excellent anthology of non-fiction written about mothers by their literary daughters. The nineteen writers, who include Simone de Beauvoir, Kim Chernin, Colette, Jean Kerr, Audre Lorde and Faye Moskowitz, represent a fairly wide range of backgrounds. The experiences here, however, are nearly all positive ones, making this more of a celebration of motherhood than an exploration of it. With this as its goal, the collection provides a density of discoveries that no single author could provide, and its optimistic, warm outlook makes this book one mothers and daughters will feel comfortable sharing with each other.

96. Caplan, Paula J. *Don't Blame Mother. Mending the Mother-Daughter Relationship.* New York: Harper & Row, 1989.

Caplan has written this book to help mothers and daughters resolve the difficulties in their relationships with each other. She begins by dismantling the myths surrounding mothers and the mother-daughter relationship, myths which limit ways of seeing themselves and each other. She also shows how mothers and daughters are socialized to act certain ways and have certain ideas about their intertwined roles. Primarily addressed to the daughter, Caplan explores our anger and how we get stuck in emotional dead-ends. She then suggests positive changes including letting go of the myths, such as mothers and "good" daughters don't get angry and that mothers are infinite nurturers. The book includes the interview questions Caplan used as well as an extensive bibliography. Portions were adopted from Caplan's earlier work, *Barriers Between Women* (1981).

97. Carlson, Kathie. *In Her Image: The Unhealed Daughter's Search for her Mother*. Boston and Shaftesbury: Shambhala, 1989.

Written from a Jungian perspective, Carlson connects contemporary problems of mothers and daughters to images from the Old Religion of the Goddess or Great Mother with the intention of enabling daughters to find meaning and understanding in their own personal experiences of mothering. The unsatisfied longings (as well as unvoiced fears, desires and angers) between mothers and daughters, she argues, are the result of the lack of the Great Mother archetype in our daily lives. From three perspectives on the Goddess: unhealed child, feminist and transpersonal—come insights which Carlson claims can be the source of wholeness for women as mothers *and* daughters. *Motherself. A Mythic Analysis of Motherhood* by Kathryn Rabuzzi (Bloomington: Indiana University, 1988) looks at mothering from a similar perspective.

98. Carter, Elizabeth, Peggy Papp, Olga Silverstein and Marianne Walters. *Mothers & Daughters: Papers Presented in Conferences.* Monograph Series, Vol. 1, No. 1. Washington D.C.: The Women's Project in Family Therapy, 1982.

This small pamphlet (38 pages) consists of four papers presented in conferences in 1981 and 1982 including "Legacies: Intergenerational Themes" which looks at how ways of relating and functioning are handed down from mothers to daughters. Carter feels the most important legacy a mother can give her daughter is the way she lives her own life and the kind of relationship she conducts with her own mother. "Fusion: The Ultimate Stalemate" examines the mother's inability to function on behalf of herself which is a problem inherent in mothering. Silverstein points out that the capacities and commitments needed for mothering are exactly those which make mothering problematic. "Rebellion: Seeds of Change" investigates the relationship between mothers and their adolescent daughters and includes a case study. Walters offers the idea that the adolescent daughter's rebellion is not so much a push for freedom but a plea for her mother to be strong and proud of herself. Finally, in "Resolutions: Together Differently" Papp agrees with Carter that the quality of a mother's life is her primary legacy to her daughter and that mothers need understanding and appreciation of what they have attempted to accomplish. This pamphlet was published by The Women's Project in Family Therapy, 2153 Newport Place, N.W., Washington, DC 20037. A later book has been published by these authors: *The Invisible Web: Gender Patterns in Family Relationships* (New York: Guilford, 1988).

99. Chesler, Phyllis. "Mothers and Daughters: A Mythological Commentary on the Lives" in *Women and Madness*. New York: Doubleday, 1972, pp. 17–24.

Chesler offers an analysis of the mother-daughter relationship and looks at how female reproductive biology, patriarchal culture and the mother-child relationship combine to ensure typical female behaviors such as submissiveness and dependency. She finds that women still choose to be wives and mothers for male-imposed reasons, such as economic survival and inadequate contraception.

Chesler points out that poets sigh over motherhood but continue their creative work; lawmakers defend motherhood in speeches but destroy its product in wars. The remainder of the book deals with the mental asylum and private therapy as mirrors of the female experience in the family and includes interviews with 60 patients between the ages of 17 and 70, most of whom were not mad but self-destructive in approved female ways.

100. Chodorow, Nancy. "Family Structure and Feminine Personality" (1973) in Michelle Rosaldo and Louise Lamphere, eds. *Women, Culture and Society*. Stanford, Calif.: Stanford University Press, 1974, pp. 46–66.

This essay pre-dates Chodorow's *The Reproduction of Mothering* (19). Like its successor, it is basically concerned with the analysis of female personality development as a result of the daughter-mother interaction in early childhood. This earlier version, though, is more deterministic in regard to women's ability to move out of their oppression. The author has been criticized (see Westkott, 131) for her lack of context in regard to patriarchy, but she does promote the idea of strong mothers rearing strong daughters, a common occurrence in matrifocal societies in which the continuing existence of the family is dependent upon the role of the mother. This essay has also been published in Chodorow's recent book *Feminism and Psychoanalytic Theory* (318).

101. Cochrane, Marybelle H. "The Mother-Daughter Dyad Throughout the Life Cycle." *Women & Therapy* 4 (Summer 1985): 3–8.

With specific emphasis on women's roles, the primary thesis of this article is on the importance of flexibility and independence in long-term mother-daughter relationships. Women's roles assume many different forms throughout the life cycle and if a daughter can feel the strength of the mother-daughter bond, through personal family history, ideology, values and beliefs, this will help to build individuality and identity. According to Cochrane, enforcement of family tradition through the mother-daughter bond is especially important in today's ever-changing face of the family.

102. Curtis (Craig), Patricia. *Why Isn't My Daughter Married? Daughters Tell Mothers the Real Reason They're Single.* Los Angeles: Price, Stern, Sloan, 1988.

Craig was one of the authors of the "Yale-Harvard Study" (1986) which projected that fewer college-educated women would marry, inadvertently receiving a blitz of media coverage. This book was written as a response in order to look at the *choices* young women are making today between marriage and careers and to eradicate the message that ambitious women were making a mistake by foregoing traditional values. Although not about mothering per se, this offers an interesting investigation of perceptions between mothers and daughters regarding the role of marriage, motherhood and work in the lives of daughters. Craig found that single, career-oriented women demand more equality from marriage than did their mothers and that this often leads to conflict between mothers and daughters. The book includes the two questionnaires, one for mothers and one for daughters, used for Craig's research as well as a short bibliography.

103. Firman, Julie, and Dorothy Firman. *Daughters and Mothers: Healing the Relationship.* New York: Continuum, 1989.

Although this book was written as a workbook with practical steps enabling mothers and daughters to heal old wounds and grow together, it has been included here because of its positive outlook toward the mother/daughter relationship. Written by a mother-daughter team of two psychotherapists who specialize in mother-daughter workshops, it includes stories, letters and comments by a variety of women, including the authors. Each section analyzes certain aspects of the mother/daughter relationship, such as messages received in the female experience of growing up and ends with a "workshop" section of exercises for mothers and daughters to try.

104. Fischer, Lucy Rose. "Transitions in the Mother-Daughter Relationship." *Journal of Marriage and the Family* 43: 3 (August 1981): 613–622.

This article incorporates some of the interviews and research Fischer used in her later book, *Linked Lives* (105). She examines the impact of the daughter's transition to mothering and motherhood on the mother-daughter relationship and finds that when daughters becomes mothers the mother and daughter re-evaluate each other and often become more involved in one another's lives.

105. Fischer, Lucy Rose. *Linked Lives: Adult Daughters and Their Mothers*. New York: Harper & Row, 1986.

Based on interviews with young adult daughters and their mothers, Fischer looks at what happens to the mother-daughter relationship when the daughter also becomes a mother. She follows the daughter from her adolescent years to being a daughter in-law into responsibility for an aging mother. Fischer uses a number of tables to illustrate comparative factors such as attachment and separation between adolescent daughters and their mothers. The most common attachment consisted of "highly involved" mothers and daughters; the most common separation was by means of implicit censorship by both the mother and daughter. This study of mothers and daughters is written from a sociological, rather than psychoanalytic viewpoint, making it more accessible to the average reader. Like many other contemporary writers, Fischer sees gender roles as being an important part of family relationships. See Price (74) and Kohler (56) for other generational studies.

106. Flax, Jane. "The Conflict Between Nurturance and Autonomy in Mother-Daughter Relationships and Within Feminism." *Feminist Studies* 4: 2 (June 1978): 171–189.

Flax feels that women want both nurturance and autonomy in intimate relationships but since development takes place in the patriarchal family, women become nurturers and men become authoritarians. The child's psychological development occurs within a socio-economic system that also strongly affects the mother. This system, along with patriarchy, impinges on her ability to provide emotional support for the child. Flax looks at anti-feminism and anti-female behavior among women as paralleling an early childhood drama of the experience of commonalty with the mother severed by a need for differentiation. This is the paradox of female development, according to Flax—over-identification with the mother masks a deep rage toward her and toward all women whereby both men and women form an alliance with a subordination to partriarchal authority. See Flax's later article on mothers and daughters, 107.

107. Flax, Jane. "Mother-Daughter Relationships: Psychodynamics, Politics and Philosophy" (1979) in Hester Eisenstein and Alice Jardine, eds. *The Future of Difference*. Boston: G.K. Hall, 1980, pp. 20–40.

Flax outlines what she believes is lacking, from a feminist viewpoint, in Freud's theory of psychological development and then illustrates, with a case study of one of her own patients, a "psycho-political analysis of patriarchal structures." Flax sees a denial of our dependence on the mother as the essential element of patriarchy and feels that current philosophy and political theory reflect the division of the world by gender. Like Chodorow (19), Flax is concerned with pre-oedipal gender identity but unlike Chodorow, she believes women are impeded by a lack of differentiation with the mother. She believes that the mother's over-identification with the daughter inhibits their separation. Her theories on the mother-daughter relationship are, although controversial, both interesting and important. See Flax's earlier article, 106.

108. Fox, Greer Litton. "The Mother-Adolescent Daughter Relationship as a Sexual Socialization Structure." *Family Relations* 29 (1980): 21–28.

This article offers a review of current analytic literature on the discussion of sex and contraception between mothers and daughters. The author has found that the transference of information between mothers and daughters re sexual behavior and conduct occurs infrequently due to influences of immediate family and society. It is also apparent that current social community programs do not look to mother-daughter relationships as a natural way of "sexual socialization."

109. Fox, Greer Litton, and Judith K. Inazu. "The Influence of Mother's Marital History on the Mother-Daughter Relationship in Black and White Households." *Journal of Marriage and Family* 44 (February 1982): 143–154.

These authors conducted a study of 449 black and white teenage daughters from a range of socioeconomic backgrounds in Detroit, Michigan in order to test these hypotheses: (1) daughters from non-intact houses would be more likely to serve as companions to their mothers (2) these same daughters would be more involved in task-sharing with their mothers and (3) they would be more responsible for their own care. The first two hypotheses were not supported and showed little difference resulting from marital status or race. In the third case, black daughters from father-absent families had significantly less adult supervision. The authors conclude that emotional aspects of relational systems rather than formal roles are the significant differentiators.

110. *Frontiers: A Journal of Women Studies.* Special Issue: Mothers and Daughters. 3: 2 (Summer 1978).

This complete issue on mothers and daughters contains a book excerpt, articles, book reviews, reminiscences, journal entries, literary criticism, fiction, poetry and a play. See Rosenberg (125), Voorhees (128) and Westkott (131) for individual articles in this issue.

Genevie, Louise, and Eva Margolies. *The Motherhood Report: How Women Feel About Being Mothers.* New York: Macmillan, 1987. See 40 for annotated entry.

111. Gilbert, Lucy, and Paula Webster. *Bound By Love: The Sweet Trap of Daughterhood.* Boston: Beacon Press, 1982.

This book examines and analyzes the socialization process of women's victimization. The question posed is not why men victimize but why women become victims. Gilbert and Webster look to daughterhood where femininity is created and oppression first occurs for the answer. The authors looked at repeated motifs of battered women who, despite fear of physical harm and feelings of worthlessness, felt bound to the men in their lives and related this to the psychological development of women. They see women's experience in the institution of daughterhood as an introduction to the two-gender system and to a recognition that violence against women is personal to us all. The internalization of the cultural construct of femininity results in a vulnerability to victimization. In becoming feminine, we are conditioned to act inferior. Therefore, violence is a result of current gender arrangements and is symbolic of women's powerlessness.

112. Hammer, Signe. *Daughters and Mothers: Mothers and Daughters*. New York: Quadrangle/New York Times Book Co., 1975.

Hammer's emphasis is on the psychological aspects of the mother-daughter relationship, taking into consideration racial, ethnic and class differences, although she primarily focuses on the middle-class. She does point out that for working-class women jobs are a means of earning money and the woman's primary role is that of housewife and mother, whereas many middle-class women perceive their careers and mothering as two distinct and equally important roles. This book is similar in style to Arcana's (92) and is readable and easy to relate to the stories of mothers and daughters. Hammer bases her research on over 75 interviews with mothers, daughters and grandmothers and includes a section of short but well-annotated notes. She finds that daughters today are changing in that they are more able than earlier generations to resolve the double message of independence/ femininity. These daughters believe they can work as well as marry and become adult women without being mothers. See Hirsch (114) for a critique of this work.

Hansen, Robert O., Mary E. Chernovetz and Warren H. Jones. "Maternal Employment and Androgyny." *Psychology of Women Quarterly* 2: 1 (Fall 1977): 76–78. See 196 for annotated entry.

113. Herman, Nini. *Too Long a Child: The Mother-Daughter Dyad.* London: Free Association Books, 1989.

This book is a therapist's complex exploration of the far-reaching impact of the mother-daughter dyad. Drawing on her experiences as daughter, mother and therapist, as well as Freudian, historical and mythological sources, Herman examines the ongoing discourse concerning the source of women's identity. Herman's thesis is that the life-long struggle for psychic mother-daughter separation is at the core of every woman's life. She not only tries to define this relationship, but also to know the nature of its pathologies and their remedies. Although critical of Freud and his followers, Herman's approach is largely psychoanalytic. Lacan is an especially important, if not central character in her discussion; Dorothy Dinnerstein (27) is also a major voice. Herman's book will most interest those already involved in this discourse, but it is accessible enough in its references to historical and mythological women to be meaningful to anyone interested in the complexity, ambivalence and power of the mother-daughter dyad.

114. Hirsch, Marianne. "Mothers and Daughters." A Review Essay. *Signs* 7: 11 (1981): 200–222.

Hirsch has written a thorough review essay of the most important mother-daughter literature published between Rich's ground-breaking *Of Woman Born* (76) in 1976 and 1981, including literary criticism, sociological and psychoanalytic texts and interview studies. Aside from the extensive section of textual analyses of literary representations of mothers and daughters, Hirsch critiques the works of Chodorow, Dinnerstein, Rich, Flax, Benjamin, Jean Baker Miller, Irigaray, Ruddick, Hammer and Arcana, all of which have been annotated herein. While showing the differences between these writers, such as degrees of responsibility of the mother for her children, Hirsch also notes the points of intersection among them, one of which is stressing the continuity between mothers and daughters. Her primary concern which can be seen throughout this essay is that a male theorist is often at the source of these feminist theories and that these writers are enmeshed in the language of patriarchy. Another essay on motherhood, unavailable for annotation, is "Perspectives on Motherhood: A Review Essay" by Rebecca Coulter (*Atlantis* 10 (September 1985): 127–137).

Hoffman, Lois W. "The Effects of Maternal Employment on The Child: A Review of the Research." *Developmental Psychology* 10: 2 (1974): 204–228. See 198 for annotated entry.

115. Irigaray, Luce. "And the One Doesn't Stir without the Other." Translated by Helene Vivienne Wenzel. *Signs* 7 (Autumn 1981): 60–67.

Irigaray believes that a feminist reciprocity between mother and daughter results in mutual empowerment but that unfortunately there is an ambivalence in the mother-daughter relationship as it exists today. Mothers and daughters are caught in a double-bind of paralysis caused by dependency, rather than inter-dependency. The daughter needs a mother to give her life while the mother retains life herself. Irigaray believes the patriarchy, as seen through Freud and Lacan, requires the separation of mothers and daughters and that we will only begin healing this split when we work toward a matriarchal ethic, that is a society which is centered around the beliefs and concerns of women. See Kuykendall's essay on Irigaray (309), Hirsch's critique (114) and Olivier for the writing of another French feminist (328).

116. Joseph, Gloria. "Mothers and Daughters: Traditional and New Perspectives." *Sage* 1: 2 (Fall 1984): 17–21.

Joseph addresses black traditional, teenage and lesbian mothers and daughters. She is quick to point out that the recent plethora of studies on mothering are inapplicable to the relationships between black mothers and daughters and are in contrast to the results of research conducted on black subjects. While Chodorow (19) and many other theorists have stated that mothering is the cause of female dependence, Joseph and other researchers she quotes state that black females are socialized by their mothers to be strong independent women. Joseph feels that mother/daughter interaction must be discussed within the context of the black family and community network (see Stack's study, 260) and that racial oppression and cultural differences are critical factors. She goes on to discuss at length the "new populations" of teenage mothers and lesbian couples with the conclusions that the adolescent mother is the result of emotional, psychological and social factors and that many lesbian couples are now choosing to have children of their own and that these two groups need tremendous support. See Joseph's book, *Common Differences*, 357.

117. Kleiman, Carol, and Catherine Kleiman. *Speaking of Sex: Mothers and Daughters.* Chicago: Bonus Books, 1987.

Written by a mother-daughter team, this book takes the interesting form of a dialogue either between the authors or another mother-daughter set. Although the varied voices speak of a range of experiences, they are too few to give a cross section. The dominant voice remains that of Carol Kleiman (the journalist-mother), and the book is therefore as idiosyncratic as her own views on sexuality. Still, it is an interesting sample of mother-daughter experiences and makes a good informal source for mothers who want to discuss sexual subjects with their daughters.

118. Lewis, Jill. "Mothers, Daughters and Feminism" in Gloria I. Joseph and Jill Lewis, eds. *Common Differences: Conflicts in Black & White Feminist Perspectives.* New York: Anchor Press/Doubleday, 1981, pp. 127–148.

This article looks at what it means to be a mother in white patriarchal society—how the images that are projected by the media of the happy nuclear family are not based on the reality of most women's lives which often encompass isolation and poverty. Lewis gives a short historical account of how women have been made to be dependent upon men and how mothers and daughters have been separated. She looks at recent writings on motherhood including Rich (76), Oakley (68–69), Chodorow (19), Tillie Olsen and Fay Weldon and at how the women's movement has tried to come to terms with the oppression of mothers and find ways to change it. Although interesting, this article is somewhat out of date and gives no recognition to contemporary feminist mothers who are currently producing strong daughters.

119. Lynn, David Brandon. *Daughters and Parents: Past, Present and Future*. Monterey, Calif.: Brooks/Cole, 1979.

Part one looks at the role of daughters throughout history and in various cultures with particular emphasis on the United States from colonial times to the present. Part two looks at the daughter's relationship with her parents and includes chapters on mothers and daughters and single mothers, as well as adolescent daughters. Part three looks at daughters today and offers an analysis of traditional femininity with the conclusion that those daughters raised to be androgynous persons are more likely to be creative, achieving women, often balancing careers and families (see Hansen and Chernovetz, 196, for similar findings). Lynn uses research current in the 1970s from sociology journals and books and includes an extensive bibliography, primarily pertaining to child development.

Millet, D.M. "Effects of Maternal Employment on Sex Role Perception, Interests and Self-Esteem in Girls." *Developmental Psychology* 11 (May 1975): 405–406. See 211 for annotated entry.

120. Neisser, Edith. *Mothers and Daughters: A Lifelong Relationship*. Rev. ed. New York: Harper & Row, 1973.

Although each relationship is unique, Neisser investigates commonalties in mother-daughter relationships as a means to help guide and reassure women in these relationships. She finds that mothers who worked out their own rebellions are more accepting of their daughter's behavior and that in white working-class families girls see their mothers as the authority figure more often than they do their fathers. Chapters on the father's and mother's influence on their daughter, the relationship between grandmothers and granddaughters, the grown daughter and her older mother, mothers and daughters in other cultures (Hopi Indian, Northern India, Israel) and in literature are included. As this book was originally published in 1967, it is pre-Chodorow and pre-feminist.

121. Notar, Margaret, and Susan A. McDaniel, eds. "Feminist Attitudes and Mother-Daughter Relationships in Adolescence." *Adolescence* 21 (September 1986): 11–21.

This study concentrated on finding the impact of feminism on mother-daughter relationships by interviewing (102) college-aged women through questionnaires. It found that the majority of young women perceived that they had a favorable relationship with their mothers and often think of both themselves and their mothers as feminists although these young women did not credit feminism "explicitly" for their good mother-daughter relationships. However, those young women who saw the relationships with their mothers as less than satisfactory held feminism somewhat accountable. The limitations to this study are great: the sample was small and limited to university students. Furthermore, only the daughters were surveyed. Although this study raises more questions than it answers, it is a useful start on an important issue.

Olivier, Christiane. *Jocasta's Children: The Imprint of the Mother*. (1980). Translated by George Kraig. London and New York: Routledge, 1989. See 328 for annotated entry.

122. Payne, Karen, ed. *Between Ourselves: Letters Between Mothers and Daughters, 1750–1982*. Boston: Houghton Mifflin, 1983.

This book is a compilation of letters from mothers to daughters and vice versa from the mid-nineteenth century to the present. Some are by well-known individuals, others by ordinary people. Payne has interspersed the letters with historical and critical information. In the case of the more contemporary communications she has actually been involved in receiving letters herself from the mother and/or daughter and uses her insights to look at the relationship. This is a book which offers a great deal of raw material for analysis. The letters are divided into sections such as "The Men in Our Lives," "Children" and "Dangerous Dreams" which are not in any particular chronological order. Contemporary writers include Jessie Bernard and Robin Morgan while earlier letters are by Helen Keller, Amelia Earhart and Sylvia Plath. There appears to be some disagreement across generations as the feminist movement has caused women to challenge traditional roles but there are also numerous examples of women who encouraged each other to go beyond the conventions of good mother and dutiful daughter.

123. Pearson, Jessica. "Mothers and Daughters: Measuring Occupational Inheritance." *Sociology and Social Research* 67: 2 : 205–217.

By using national samples of whites and blacks, Pearson looked at patterns of female, intergenerational, occupational transmission by means of three different measures of female inheritance: gains or losses in status indicated by a women when her own occupational status is compared with that of her father's, when her husband's occupational status is compared with that of her father's and when her own occupational status is compared with that of her mother's. Traditional studies used only the first two comparisons whereas recent surveys have begun to include questions about mothers' occupations. It was found that for both races, the mother's occupational status was significantly associated with that of her daughter's. The influences of mothers on daughters generally exceeded the influence of fathers on daughters, fathers on the spouses of daughters and in the case of blacks, that of the fathers on sons. Pearson notes that these results must be viewed tentatively as the data were originally collected in 1966. Still, it is interesting to see the obvious trend of working mothers' influence on their children.

Price, Jane. *Motherhood: What It Does To Your Mind.* London: Pandora Press, 1988. See 74 for annotated entry.

124. Rollins, Judy, and Priscilla N. White. "The Relationship Between Mothers' and Daughters' Sex-Role Attitudes and Self-Concepts in Three Types of Family Environment." *Sex Roles* 8: 11 (1982): 1141–1155.

Since it is assumed that mothers are usually significant others in daughters' socialization, this study was conducted to see if significant relationships exist between mothers and daughters regarding sex-role attitudes and self-concepts. Three types of families were sampled: first, the mother was a full-time homemaker, second, she was employed due to economic necessity and third, she was employed for personal and professional fulfillment. It was found that mothers and daughters do share similar views on certain sex-role variables. For example, mothers and daughters in dual-career families had more non-traditional attitudes regarding marriage than mothers and daughters in the other two groups. However, these daughters were not rejecting marriage but viewing it from a more egalitarian perspective. It should be noted that daughters of traditional mothers chose the option of "wife, mother, and career" as frequently as daughters in the other two groups, although there was a relatively high number (24%) of dual-career daughters who reported that they would choose marriage and careers only as future roles. This study found no difference between the self-concept scores of the three groups of mothers and daughters which is in direct contrast to Hoffmann's findings (200) wherein dual-career women were the most satisfied in both personal and work roles.

125. Rosenberg, Jan, and Sarah Gallagher. "Mothers and Daughters: A Seminar for Older Returning College Students." *Frontiers: A Journal for Women Studies* 3: 2 (1978): 22–27.

The topic of mothers and daughters allows these professors to incorporate their interests in sociology and literature with the life experiences of older students. This is a description of the seminar and the readings that were used as well as a synopsis of the resulting students work. One student produced an annotated bibliography on mothers and daughters and a woman with adolescent daughters investigated the mother-daughter relationship in adolescent fiction. The article includes a good bibliography on mothers and daughters, covering both fiction and nonfiction works.

126. *Sage*. Special Issue: Mothers and Daughters. 1: 2 (Fall 1984).

This early number is the first of two issues on the subject of mothers and daughters. It contains a series of retrospective analyses by three daughters (including Bell Hooks), a mother and grandmother, a photographic essay, a study on teenage motherhood and a review of mother-daughter relationships in black women's fiction. A two-page list of readings relating to the subject, which includes books, research reports, articles, dissertations and theses, is also included. Although many of the references are concerned with teenage pregnancy and quite a few others are annotated herein, this is a valuable resource for works on black mothers. One article by Gloria Joseph has been annotated separately (see 116). The second issue of *Sage* devoted to mothers and daughters (4: 2 Fall 1987) contains one article on mother-daughter relationships by Patricia Hill Collins with the remainder consisting of literary criticism, narratives, documents, poetry and fiction).

127. Sholomskas, Diane, and Rosalind Axelrod. "The Influence of Mother-Daughter Relationships on Women's Sense of Self and Current Role Choices." *Psychology of Women's Quarterly* 10: (1986): 171–182.

This article investigates the relationship between women's current role choices, role satisfaction and self-esteem to their perceptions of their mothers' role choices and role satisfaction. It is based on interviews and self-report inventories with 67 married women with pre-school children, 28 of whom had a career, 12 worked outside the home and 27 were homemakers. The authors found that daughters are more influenced by their mothers' feelings about their own work than by their actual role choice. Other significant findings included the positive relation between women's self-esteem and strong ties with their mother, working mothers as providing their daughters with less female stereotyped values and that career women were the most satisfied with their primary role choices (see Hoffman, 200, for similar findings and Rollins, 124, for contrasting ones). It also noted that a larger percentage of the homemakers perceived their mothers as positive role models, which correlates with Gerson's (42) investigation of the negative relation between feminism and mothering.

128. Voorhees, Sara. Review of *My Mother/Myself: The Daughter's Search for Identity* in *Frontiers: A Journal of Women Studies.* 3: 2 (Summer 1978): 75–76.

Voorhees points out the basic flaws of Nancy Friday's book, particularly its mother-blaming tone and its perpetuation of the myth that a woman is nothing without a man. She compares it to Rich's *Of Woman Born* (76) which Voorhees believes has a much deeper and positive analysis of the mother-daughter relationship. Hirsch (114) also critiques this book.

129. Walker, Alexis J., Linda Thompson and Carolyn Stout Morgan. "Two Generations of Mothers and Daughters: Role Position and Independence." *Psychology of Women Quarterly* 11: 2 (1987): 195–208.

A survey of a 135 pairs of women students and their mothers and 119 pairs of the same middle-aged mothers and their own mothers was conducted to see how a woman's role position interacts with her partner's role position in regard to interdependence. It was found that interdependence was remarkably unrelated to role positions. In the younger pairs, only the daughter's marital status emerged as connected with interdependence wherein single daughters and their mothers were more closely related than married daughters. It is also interesting that in the younger mother-daughter pairs the dependent member reported less attachment than the non-dependent member. This study, although quite complex, indicates the changing nature of the mother-daughter bond and the connection between material and emotional interdependence. For further information see an earlier article on the subject by Thompson and Walker, "Mothers and Daughters: Aid Patterns and Attachment" in *Journal of Marriage and the Family* (May 1984).

130. Weeks, M. O'Neal, George W. Wise and Charlotte Duncan. "The Relationship between Sex-Role Attitudes and Career Orientations of High School Females and their Mothers." *Adolescence* 19 (Fall 1984): 595–607.

This study looks at the relationship between sex-role attitudes of secondary school females and their mothers in three areas: the daughter's career plans, the mother's career status and the grandmother's career status. It is surprising to see that out of the four career status differentiations, including full-time homemaker, homemaker with part-time employment, homemaker with full-time employment and career women, the most pro-feminist attitudes amongst both the mothers and the daughters were encountered among the homemakers with part-time employment. Generally, the daughters' career plans were not closely related to the career status of their mothers or grandmothers and they tended to reflect less homemaker-type aspirations.

131. Westkott, Marcia. "Mothers and Daughters in the World of the Father." *Frontiers: A Journal of Women Studies* 3: 2 (1978): 16–20.

Westkott analyzes mothers and daughters in relation to their roles in the patriarchy, as do other writers, such as Lewis (118) and Rich (76). She feels that the role of the father is a debatable point when studying single mothers and daughters (see Mitchell's analysis, 327, for a similar view). Westkott gives a good explanation of Chodorow's (19) theories of female personality development while criticizing her for resigning herself to women's oppression and not understanding its connection to patriarchy. She looks at Chodorow's work in relation to that of Rich and says that Rich's work "offers the critical perspective and alternative vision to motherhood in the patriarchy that Chodorow's lacks."

132. Wodak, Ruth, and Muriel Schulz *The Language of Love and Guilt: Mother-Daughter Relationships from a Cross-Cultural Perspective*. Amsterdam and Philadelphia: J. Benjamins, 1986.

Written from a sociological-psychological perspective, Wodak and Schulz have completed a comparison of mother/daughter relationships between women living in Vienna and Los Angeles, with particular emphasis on linguistic implications. Love and guilt refer to two of the cross-cultural similarities between mothers and daughters found in the study. The primary difference which surfaced was that American daughters, at least on the surface, appeared to have less conflict with their mothers than their European counterparts.

Women's Studies Quarterly. Special Issue: Teaching About Mothering. 11: 4 (Winter 1983). See 89 for annotated entry.

133. Yalom, Marilyn, Suzanne Estler and Wenda Brewster. "Changes in Female Sexuality: A Study of Mother/Daughter Communication and Generational Differences." *Psychology of Women Quarterly* 7: 2 (Winter 1982): 141–153.

This study was conducted through questionnaires of 141 women who graduated from college in 1954 and currently had college-age daughters and 184 young women who were sophomores at university in 1977–1978. It was found that although major changes in sexual behavior have occurred within affluent and well-educated families, there is no evidence of a backlash by mothers in this class against the greater sexual freedom of their daughters and that these mothers and daughters expressed similar attitudes toward sex, although the daughters tended to be somewhat more liberal. The communication between mothers and daughters on the subject of sex seems to have improved over the past 25 years but it should be noted that the women in this study were generally from middle- and upper-class families with close, stable relationships. It is interesting to note that 90% of the mothers said that they would feel negative if their daughters were to establish a homosexual relationship while only 78% of the daughters expressed comparable sentiments.

134. Zamir, Aviva. *Mothers and Daughters: Interviews with Kibbutz Women*. Norwood, Pa.: Norwood Editions, 1986.

Zamir interviews women who are the "finished product" of kibbutz education and who now have children themselves. She examines the lack of equality between the sexes, despite an ideology of equality, and looks at the status of women within kibbutz society to see how this is changing, if at all, in the younger generation. She finds little progress has been made toward creating a more egalitarian society. See Kitzinger (55) for other research on the kibbutz.

III.

Mothers and Sons: A New Frontier

In comparison to the subject of mothers and daughters, the literature on mothers and sons is scant. With the exception of feminist women such as Audre Lorde and Judith Arcana who are bringing up sons, there has been little interest in the subject. Obviously, there should be; unless men change, the whole patriarchal system will never be completely eliminated. But this means it is incumbent on the parents of boys to take responsibility for raising their sons with a feminist perspective.

Mothers who wish to bring up daughters to believe they can accomplish anything they want have an exciting task. Mothers who wish to bring up feminist sons in a patriarchal society have a daunting challenge. Most of the authors of these few books agree that mothers need to teach their sons that it is patriarchal society and not women at whom they should direct their anger. Carole Klein (137), who looks at the subject from a psychological perspective, points out that sons must differentiate from their mothers at the same time as retaining their initial closeness. Sons must be taught not to fear the love of women.

Besides a need to separate from their mothers in order to identify with a masculine gender, boys are constantly bombarded with masculine, Rambo-type imagery as well as anti-woman propaganda. When a young boy who is being raised with feminist ideals starts school he is confronted with peers who are already dismissive of girls. He must have a strong sense of self to be able to withstand the teasing and bullying which he will certainly encounter if he acts differently. Sandra Bem (283) offers some innovative ideas for raising "gender-aschematic" children beginning with the parents reducing their own sex-typed behavior.

Chodorow's chapter "Sexual Sociology" in *The Reproduction of Mothering* (19) studies the development of boys in relation to their mothers. She feels that most mothers do not have the same problem separating from their sons as from their daughters. According to Chodorow, this could be because boys tend to deny the affective relationship with their mothers in order to proceed in their identification with a masculine gender, but what if there is no male who is continuously present? Or what if the father is seriously participating in the parenting process? These are just a few of the questions which need to be addressed and which could hold the answers for change.

According to Klein and Arcana, mothers are ambivalent about their sons. They are afraid of creating a "Mama's boy" and will often bring up their daughters to be more like boys than they do their sons to have the female qualities of empathy and nurturance. Arcana (135) elucidates an important issue: mothers of sons must realize that they are involved in raising their own and their daughters' oppressors. It appears from the literature that feminist mothers are more conscious than traditional mothers of the need for sharing activities and teaching their sons what they perceive to be female strengths. Klein found that grown sons of feminist mothers are also interested in women with whom they can have an equal partnership.

Finally, what about the mothers of these sons, how do they look at their roles, particularly from a feminist viewpoint within the current patriarchal system? Klein and Linda Forcey (136) look at how it feels for a woman to be the mother of a male child. They found that women often speak to men, including their sons, in a different voice than they use for their daughters. This voice stems from a double-edged fear of holding their sons too close at the same time as being afraid of letting go and losing them forever. One interesting finding on which Klein and Forcey differ is the mother's concern for her son's worldly success as opposed to her daughter's. Unlike Klein, Forcey found that mothers do not always have great expectations for their sons. This phenomenon is also seen in some studies of black matriarchal families whereby the mother puts more energy in bringing up her daughter, who she believes will eventually have to take care of herself and her family (see Diane Lewis, 259).

Two other books, *Sons and Mothers* (142) and *Raising Sons* (143), lean toward holding the mother responsible for her son's development and behavior. They have been included because there are so few books on the subject and as examples of well-intentioned works that are probably widely read yet which are not particularly helpful in changing the socialization process of boys into men.

Hope for the future may lie with the sons of feminist mothers. These young men will have the opportunity and probably the power as well to initiate changes in the workplace so that their self-chosen familial responsibilities can be met.

BIBLIOGRAPHY— MOTHERS AND SONS

135. Arcana, Judith. *Every Mother's Son*. Garden City, N.Y.: Doubleday, 1983.

Arcana has based her second book (see the previous section for her work on mothers and daughters, 91–92) on interviews with sixty mothers and sons as well as her own experience as a mother of a young son. Arcana looks at the problem of mothers raising sons in a world where men are encouraged to degrade women. Feminist mothers want to raise sons to be different, yet they do not want them to be ostracized by a society which is not ready to change. This underscores the points that it is not enough for only women to change nor is equality with men an appropriate goal. Although Arcana found that many mothers of sons were afraid to influence the male character and were afraid of being blamed for their sons' behavior, she states that it is necessary for mothers of sons to examine the patterns in society which produce insensitive, violent men. We must understand that we are raising our own and our daughters' oppressors. Mothers of sons must find the balance between supporting their sons' developing selves while undermining the power of male supremacy.

Bem, Sandra L. "Gender Schema Theory and Its Implications for Child Development: Raising Gender-aschematic Children in a Gender-schematic Society." *Signs* 8: 4 (Summer 1983): 598–616.

See 283 in Section VIII on The Children for a full annotation of this article which is relevant to the raising of both sons and daughters.

136. Forcey, Linda Rennie. *Mothers of Sons: Toward an Understanding of Responsibility*. New York: Praeger, 1987.

Forcey, who states that she wishes to contribute to feminist theory as a social scientist, points out that pre-feminist scholarship dealt with the effect (always negative) of the mother on the son, never on how having a son affected the mother or how the mother could have a positive effect on her son. The focus of this book is on mother-son relationships from the perspective of the mothers. It is based on oral histories of over 100 women between the ages of 36 and 55 from a range of socio-economic backgrounds. Forcey's main questions were how do mothers perceive their relationships with sons, is this different from daughters, is it affected by the mother's attitude toward men and what variables, such as class, etc., affect these perceptions. Forcey's findings include the following: (1) both conventional and revised feminist ideas of the responsibility of mothers for sons are harmful to both men and women because they ignore the effect of society on the male child; (2) women speak in a different voice to their sons which is not their usual "different" voice, i.e., caring, but which is often conciliatory due to a fear of confrontation; (3) many working-class mothers of post-adolescent sons wanted them to join the military because the mothers were overwhelmed with responsibility for their son's lives and (4) mothers do not invariably have great expectations for their sons. In fact, Forcey found that they are much more concerned with worldly success for their daughters. This is in contrast to Carol Klein's findings (137).

Genevie, Louise, and Eva Margolies. *The Motherhood Report: How Women Feel About Being Mothers*. New York: Macmillan, 1987. See 40 for annotated entry.

137. Klein, Carol. *Mothers and Sons*. Boston: Houghton Mifflin, 1984.

Interviews with over 30 psychiatrists and psychologists, a thorough research of the professional literature and a combination questionnaire/interview with 200 men and 500 women form the basis of this book. It includes chapters on feminist mothers, lesbian mothers and homosexual sons, mothers of troubled and successful sons. The focus is on what it is like for a woman to mother a male child and what it feels like for a man to be mothered by a woman. Forcey feels the main conflict is that both the mother and son wish to stay close to one another but the mother is afraid of creating a "mama's boy" and the son needs to differentiate as a male. Generally, mothers do more to make girls like boys but feminist mothers appear to be more apt to share activities with their sons. The sons of many feminist mothers want to marry women they perceive as their equals and the mothers of these sons want to share with them what they see as their female strengths. Although the relationship of the mother and son often involves issues of power, status and sexuality, it would appear that feminist mothers raising sons have the opportunity and the challenge of creating positive changes in gender roles. In contrast to Forcey (136), Klein found that mothers were often more concerned with their son's success than that of their daughter.

138. Leon, Manuel. "Rules Mothers and Sons Use to Integrate Intent and Damage Information in Their Moral Judgments." *Child Development* 55 (1984): 2106–2113.

Although this article is quite technical in content, it has been included because of the dearth of literature on mothers and sons. A highly significant similarity was found between rules used by mothers and their sons in terms of punitive actions.

139. Longabough, Richard. "Mother Behavior as a Variable Moderating the Effects of Father Absence." *Ethos* 1: 4 (1973): 456–465.

This article focuses on the psychological and behavioral development of boys in the mother-son relationship when the father is absent. It concludes that the mother's behavior toward her son can affect the femininity of his semantic style.

Evidently, the closer the mother-son relationship, the less masculine the son's semantic style.

140. Lorde, Audre. *Sister Outsider: Essays and Speeches*. New York: The Crossing Press, 1984, pp. 72–80.

"Man Child" is an essay on Lorde's son which is beautifully presented and tells of particular problems inherent to racism and patriarchy in raising a son by a black lesbian. It relates to all mothers and sons since mothers must raise sons to see that it is the patriarchal structure, rather than mothers, that should be the object of their son's hostility.

141. Maloney, Mercedes Lynch, and Anne Maloney *The Hand that Rocks the Cradle: Mothers, Sons, & Leadership*. Englewood Cliffs, N.J.: Prentice-Hall, 1985.

The authors point out that society's attitude toward mothers and motherhood is ambivalent as mothers are viewed with deference at the same time they are dismissed. They conclude that no one has yet fully appreciated the role of the mother in her child's life (although I think Chodorow would disagree with this). They include stories of mothers whose power and influence indirectly changed our world including mothers of a number of American presidents as well as Churchill, Hitler, Marx and Freud among others. Sigmund Freud often said that his mother's "adoration" was the reason for his self-confidence and need to achieve. Karl Marx, like Freud, was the eldest of many children and his mother's favorite, although he separated from her ideologically when he was still young. Hitler's father died when he was 13 and his mother supported him until well into adulthood. The authors blame Hitler's mother for not forcing him to assume responsibility for his life so that, consequently, he always looked for scapegoats to blame for his problems. Alice Miller in *For Your Own Good* (292) gives a more insightful analysis of Hitler's life, focusing on his father's brutality toward him.

142. Olsen, Paul. *Sons and Mothers*. New York: M. Evans, 1981.

Written from the man's point of view, Olsen says that he is attempting to heal the rift between sons and their mothers and diminish the mythology surrounding the "good mother" vs. "bad mother." Nevertheless, he does indulge in some mother-blaming in his chapter on "good" and "bad" mothers. This book must be read closely because although Olsen is careful to applaud mothers who give their sons freedom and imagination (the "unsafe" mother), he sees "safe" mothers, who bring up their sons in a traditional manner, as needing to be freed from their own roles. Olsen uses very few references in his writing to back up his ideas that mothers, as opposed to fathers, are responsible for macho behavior in their sons or that mothers tend to keep fathers out of the mother-son world.

143. Rodgers, Joann Ellison, and Michael Cataldo. *Raising Sons: Practical Strategies for Single Mothers.* New York: American Library, 1984.

The authors advocate for what they call "behavioral parenting," consisting of monitoring and altering the son's behavior by watching for clues. They discuss issues such as the circumstances that have led to single motherhood and concerns over what it means to raise someone to be masculine. The authors try to take a progressive attitude toward the sexuality of both mother and son. For example, they acknowledge and explore the ambivalence single mothers may feel toward men, as well as the possibilities for raising a non-sexist son. However, assumptions about the nature of men and women appear in everything from the general boys-will-be-boys tone to the assertion that boys are naturally more aggressive and better equipped for math and science than girls. The question of whether single mothers cause their sons to be gay is repeatedly answered with an objective and emphatic "no" that might easily be interpreted as homophobic (the implication being that homosexuality is not the mother's *fault*). The possibility of a lesbian mother is not mentioned. In the end, the problem with this well-intentioned book may be its relegation of the mother to a reactive role, casting her as the manipulative woman grappling with her active son.

IV.

Single Mothers: One-Parent Children

Robert Weiss defines a single parent as one who has unshared responsibility for the care and direction of the children (174, p. xi). Anita Shreve takes this definition even further by pointing out that a single mother, unless she is on welfare or receiving ample alimony, is by necessity a working mother (223, p. 193).

The phenomenon of the single-parent family is growing. Between 1970 and 1985 these families increased by 126 percent in the United States, from a total of 12.9% to 26.3% including all races. Single-parent black families increased in this same period from 35.7 percent to 60.1 percent (U.S. Dept. of Commerce. 1986. Current Population Reports, Series P-20 #411). Since the vast majority of single-parent families are headed by women, one can interpret research in this area of family relations as particularly pertaining to women. There are numerous publications including "how-to" books, *Momma, The Newspaper Magazine For Single Mothers* and literature from support groups that are evidence of the increasing numbers of single mothers.

Many of the studies done on single mothers are tied in with studies of the children of these parents and have therefore been included here. There is some cross-over between this section and the section on children. Early studies of children of divorce assumed that any problems such as delinquency, aggression, etc., were due to the divorce without taking into consideration other factors, such as poverty (see Bilge and Kaufman, 146). In the current journal literature are the often repeated findings that the effects of poverty are much greater than those of father absence on the single-parent family and that family harmony is more important than father absence for the child (see Bilge and Kaufman, 146, Colleta, 152 and Weiss, 174). As one mother stated in Shreve's *Remaking Motherhood*, "Our home is not broken. It is very much intact" (223, p. 502).

The consensus is it's o.k. to be a single mother. Nancy Chodorow, in fact, cites studies supporting single mothering (19, p. 74). It might be that the male figure is not necessary for differentiation, that the child who is raised by a primary caretaker with a good sense of self will separate as a matter of course. Gloria Joseph points out in *Common Differences* (257) that it is the quality of the relationships within the family which are crucial to its functioning, not the actual structure. Therefore, the single-parent family may function as well as or some times even better than the dual-parent family due to strong bonding patterns and supportive social networks (see Weiss, 175, Bilge and Kaufman, 146, and Brown et al., 150).

Supportive networks are one of the primary systems affecting single mothers. Many articles and books discuss these networks as being the key to the single mother's success. Besides those noted above are articles by Michael Smith (173) and Nancy Gladow and Margaret Ray (156). "How well we do anything directly depends on the economic and social environment in which we do it," states one poor single mother (Valeska, 250, p. 71). In Sally Bould's study (147) on black and white single mothers the women dependent on stigmatizing sources of income were less sufficient and had less sense of self-worth than women able to support themselves.

Financial stability, the mother's personality and strength, availability of good day care, extended kinship or families, all of these are apparently more crucial for the single-parent family than for the nuclear. Jane Lazarre poignantly asks, "Was it possible . . . that the simple fact of a good day care center . . . was the essence of all the liberation which I had mistakenly sought in the unraveling of all of my spiritual and emotional tangles" (58, p. 158).

Carol Brown and her colleagues (150) report that if financially secure, women are often better off divorced because their lives are less restricted. And Louise Genevie and Eva Margolies found in *The Motherhood Report* (40) that mothers' relationships with their children improved as conflict over child-raising issues decreased. Therefore, the single mother might have the opportunity to become closer to her children because the lack of spouse can allow for better interaction. This increased closeness results not only from more time spent together but also from broader fields of interchange, e.g., the mother and child share more responsibility in a less hierarchal relationship. Even in terms of working mothers, the single mother may be able to devote more attention to her children than married women because of the lack of competition for her time.

A less tangible effect on single mothers reported by Pat Keith and Robert Schafer (160) results from attitudes about appropriate roles for men and women both at home and in the workplace. Women who encounter less traditional views from their employers and their spouses fare better. Women's views about themselves are also a determinant of their well-being. Those women who view the adult role as more androgynous (see Shreve, 223 and Hoffman, 198) suffer less from feelings of inadequacy as single mothers.

One of the specific problems that single mothers often encounter is in their relationships with their daughters. An interesting question that has not been sufficiently addressed is whether it is more likely for a single mother to have a narcissistic cathexis (see Alice Miller, 291) with her child, particularly if she is emotionally disabled as the result of divorce. Does a single mother generally have a harder time letting go of her daughter than does a married woman or is it easier for her, given the strong bonding that might have taken place? Evelyn Bassoff (94) addresses this issue and reaches positive conclusions, at least when the mother's attitude toward herself is one of self-confidence.

Other studies, including those by Weiss, show that single-parented children will insist the parent respect their move to autonomy because they've always been given so much freedom and responsibility. Chodorow says that women with a strong sense of self and the support of other women can create autonomous daughters, although it is her belief that girls without fathers often do not separate as well as those from two-parent families (19, pp. 212–213).

The single mothers interviewed by Judith Barker for her dissertation had many positive things to say about their lives (see fn. 1, p. xi). The consensus was that they had become empowered by the responsibility of taking care of themselves and their children. Out of the experience of being marginal in our society, these women developed alternative definitions of themselves.

Jean Renvoize (169) also found mostly happy, fulfilled women in the single mothers she interviewed. These women, though, were single mothers by choice; they were unmarried women who made a decision to become pregnant or adopt. This is a major factor when studying single mothers, probably a more important variable than race or class. Two other books focus on this type of single mother: *And Baby Makes Two* by Sharyne Merritt and Linda Steiner (168) and *The Single Parent Experience* by Carole Klein (161). Of course this relatively recent phenomenon is obviously related to class and race as primarily white middle- and upper-class women are the only ones actually choosing to become single mothers, as opposed to becoming one by default (teen-age pregnancy) or choosing to divorce after children are born. The women who are financially able to choose single parenting are probably more satisfied than even the married career mothers in Baruch's (297) scale of personal levels of happiness and control.

Yet Mark Fine and his colleagues (154) found that of mothers who had *not* chosen from the outset to become single, black single mothers were more satisfied with their lives than white ones because they perceived their experience more positively. There is still a great deal of social stigma attached to white middle-class single parents which affects both the children and the mothers. According to Roy Austin (252), there is a stronger relationship between father absence and involvement in personal offenses, such as running away and truancy, for white girls than for any other group. The lack of a father in lower socio-economic homes may actually be conducive to strong mother-daughter bonds since mothers and daughters living alone have more impetus to turn to each other for support, although a study by Greer Litton Fox and Judith Inazu (109) does not support this contention. However, it has been found "that the mother's affection is significantly related to delinquency for all girls" (Austin, 252, p. 502) meaning that a strong mother-daughter bond results in better behavior of daughters.

One of the positive effects on children is the nonhierarchal structure that often exists in single-parent families. Due to having a voice in decision-making, these children often willingly take on more responsibility. As a result, says Weiss, the children in single-parent households become more self-reliant.

> The single-parent family, in so far as it requires the children within it to behave responsibly, may, in this respect, be a better setting for growing up than the two-parent family (175, p. 110).

Barbara Bilge and Gladis Kaufman (146) also feel that the single-parent family is more supportive to children, as long as it is economically and socially stable.

Single mothers function outside the norm of society, without direct masculine interference, possibly possessing the means of changing first the family and then society. The point is not to break up the family but to change it as it exists under patriarchy, i.e., mother at home, father at work. According to Chodorow, if women raise daughters who want to become mothers, then single mothers, by combining the traditional roles of mother and father, may provide their daughters with more than just a capacity for nurturance. In terms of sons, single mothers may be the perfect solution to creating feminist men. Sons growing up without the influence of a dominant male in the family who reflects patriarchal society might be able to separate from the mother without renouncing her nurturant, i.e., female, qualities.

The problem for one-parented children and their parents is that even though over one-half of American children will spend at least some time in one-parent homes (Skolnick, 280, p. 102), schools and employers have not adjusted to this fact. Many businesses make it difficult for the single parent to miss work when her child is ill and relatively few schools offer before and after school programs to provide care for children of single working parents, who often are away from home for long hours.

The time that the single parent needs away from the children in order to support them can be a problem. As noted before, Bilge and Kaufman found that it is not the family structure that is at fault, but the economic inequalities of many single families which cause strain. Therefore, it stands to reason that if single-parent families were adequately supported, then both the mothers and the children would be better off.

The current literature on single mothers raises various questions which need to be addressed. Does the single-mother experience change the attitudes of working- or lower-class families that are historically more traditional in their outlook? Mothers usually have more involvement than fathers with children and may use affection (female) more than power (male) in directing their children. Does this change when the single mother is the sole provider and disciplinarian? Finally, Juliet Mitchell (327) says that in patriarchy the rule of the father is present even when the father himself is absent. Is this always so, and how can it be changed?

The following articles, which were unavailable for annotation, may be of interest:

Bloom, B.L., and C. Clement. "Marital Sex Role Orientation and Adjustment to Separation and Divorce." *Journal of Divorce* 7: 3 (1984): 87–98.

Gongla, Patricia. "Single-Parent Families: A Look at Families of Mothers and Children." *Marriage and Family Review* 5: 2 (1982): 5–27.

Mitchell, K. "The Price Tag of Responsibility: A Comparison of Divorced and Remarried Mothers." *Journal of Divorce* 6: 3 (1983): 33–42.

Thompson, Edward, and Patricia Gongla. "Single-Parent Families: In the Mainstream of American Society" in E. Macklin and R. Rubin, eds. *Contemporary Families and Alternative Lifestyles*. Beverly Hills: Sage, 1983.

BIBLIOGRAPHY—
SINGLE MOTHERS

144. Arendale, Terry. *Mothers & Divorce: Legal, Economic and Social Dilemmas*. Berkeley: University of California Press, 1986.

Arendale begins by dismantling popular notions about divorce, then looks at legal experiences and economic consequences. Popular literature and film show the divorce situation as either temporary or a chance for a creative new life, not as the desperate economic consequences it creates for most women, says Arendale. The author feels that divorce acts as a control on married women and has based this book on interviews with 60 divorced mothers who, as working mothers, have been economically abandoned by husbands and society. It includes an extensive bibliography and is primarily concerned with gender bias in divorce and the downward mobility of women. See Weitzman (176) for another study on the effects of divorce.

145. Barber, Dulan, ed. *One Parent Families*. London: Davis-Poynter, 1975.

Written under the auspices of the National Council for One Parent Families in London, this is a collection of personal essays and letters written by single parents and their children telling their own stories as well as a few government reports on single parenting. These stories are moving and reflect a positive, although difficult life situation.

Bassoff, Evelyn. *Mothers and Daughters: Loving and Letting Go*. New York: New American Library, 1988. See 94 for annotated entry.

146. Bilge, Barbara, and Gladis Kaufman. "Children of Divorce and One-Parent Families: A Cross Cultural Perspective." *Family Relations* 32: 1 (1983): 59–71.

The authors of this article have examined one-parent families across the globe and offer the conclusion that many are functioning very well. They point out that the one-parent family is not inherently inferior or pathological. In fact, when given supportive social networks and material resources the one-parent family has the possibility of offering more support to children than the traditional nuclear family (see Weiss, 175 for a similar view). The authors point out that the negative reports about one-parent families are often the result of social inequalities in our present society, not the fact of single parenting. They have used cross-cultural comparisons to show that marital conflict rather than marital dissolution has more of an adverse effect upon children. The authors give a number of references to other articles on the subject and point out that there are numerous studies which show that poor mothering and faulty fathering exist to an equal extent in nuclear families. They also show how different research methodologies result in different conclusions.

Birns, Beverly, and Dale Hay, eds. *The Different Faces of Motherhood*. New York: Plenum Press, 1988. See 10 for annotated entry.

147. Bould, Sally. "Female-Headed Families: Personal Fate Control and the Provider Role." *Journal of Marriage and the Family* 39: 2 (1977): 339–349.

This article examines black and white female heads of families to see how the source as well as the amount of income they received affected them. It was found that women depending on welfare and child-support and other unstable or stigmatizing sources of income felt less in control of their lives as compared to mothers who became the family provider through earned income. The author suggests a national policy of social insurance to cover the risk of family breakup as a solution to both aspects of the problem (see Bane, 262, for a similar idea).

148. Brandwein, Ruth. "After Divorce: A Focus on Single-Parent Families." *Urban and Social Change Review* 10: 1 (1977): 21–25.

This is a positively written article that strongly speaks out against the assumption that divorce is a result of "women's lib." It views divorce as a situation that can work well, contrary to popular stereotypes which attach the stigma of the "broken home" to divorce. It reviews a number of policy implications which could arise, depending on how a particular society views divorce, such as education, child-care and job training issues.

149. Brandwein, Ruth, Carol A. Brown and Elizabeth M. Fox. "Women and Children Last: The Social Situation of Divorced Mothers and their Families." *Journal of Marriage and the Family* 36 (1974): 498–514.

This article focuses on the mother and family unit which remains after the father leaves and emphasizes the consequences to the woman. The authors conclude that the women's movement (in 1974) has provided much documentation about discrimination against women but has not focused on the single mother. This, of course, has been rectified in recent years. The authors look at the need for research on the economic consequences of single parenting, the stigmatization of the single mother and the functions and roles in the single-parent family as differing from the traditional family, such as the lessening of hierarchal structures. See Brandwein's later article, 149, as well as one by Brown et.al., 150.

150. Brown, Carol A., Roslyn Feldberg, Elizabeth M. Fox and Janet Cohen. "Divorce: Chance of A Lifetime." *Journal of Social Issues* 32: 1 (1976): 119–133.

Written from a feminist perspective, these authors conclude that, with the help of support networks, single parenthood may actually be beneficial to many women (see Boulton, 11; Bilge and Kaufman, 146; and Weiss, 174). "It is a viable, even preferred life pattern for an increasing number of divorced mothers." Based on interviews with 30 divorced women, the authors look at the wife/mother package and conclude that if a woman has enough financial and emotional support she is often better off divorced, due to less restrictive domestic routines and more control over her life. These ideas, of course, imply radical changes in current social policies.

151. Buehler, Cheryl, and Janice Hogan. "Managerial Behavior and Stress in Families Headed by Divorced Women." *Family Relations* 29: 4 (1980): 525–532.

These authors look at economic stresses and their effect on the managerial patterns in female-headed families. They examine the connection between stress and poverty and investigate the resources which are or should be available to single parents. They conclude that the level of stress in female-headed families is primarily related to the exterior environment including the courts, welfare services, job opportunities and support networks. Therefore, stress can be created or reduced by systems outside the family as well as by the family's own internal management capabilities.

152. Colletta, Nancy Donahue. "The Impact of Divorce: Father Absence or Poverty?" *Journal of Divorce* 3: 1 (1979): 27–35.

The author has studied 72 single mothers to ascertain whether differences in childrearing methods are due to low income or lack of a father. The conclusion she offers is that low income is the key factor in family problems subsequent to divorce.

153. Dornbusch, Sanford M., and Kathryn Gray. "Single-Parent Families" in Sanford Dornbusch and Myra Strober, eds. *Feminism: Children and the New Families.* New York: Guilford, 1988, pp. 274–296.

This essay offers an examination of the processes that produce the problems encountered by single-parent families. These processes include the forms of family decision-making, styles of parenting and family participation in schooling. The authors point out that poverty is not the only problem for single parents (although single-mother families living in poverty range from 54% white to 70 % black). Various statistics noted include: 1/2 of American children live in single-parent homes at some point, 1/5 do so at any given time, over 50% of marriages end in divorce, 3/4 of divorced women and 5/6 of divorced men remarry, 90% of single-parent families are headed by women and the modal form of black family life is a single parent family.

154. Fine, Mark, Andrew Schwebeland and Linda Myers. "The Effect of World View on Adaptation to Single Parenthood Among Middle-Class Adult Women." *Journal of Family Issues* 6: 1 (1985): 107–127.

These authors have found that single mothers of all races who have an Afrocentric world view (i.e., more communal) rather than a Eurocentric perspective (i.e., more individualistic) were more satisfied at being mothers in a single-parent situation. In contrast to other authors (Weiss 174, Renvoize 169, etc.) they found that mothers from dual-parent families were somewhat more well adjusted.

155. Garfinkel, Irwin, and Sara S. McLanahan. *Single Mothers And Their Children: A New American Dilemma*. Washington, D.C.: Urban Institute Press, 1986.

The authors see "the new American dilemma" as the desire to provide economic security to single-parent families coupled with the need to stem their growth and dependence on government services. They believe that public assistance to mothers fosters long-term welfare dependence, marriage instability and out-of-wedlock births. Although they do not believe the welfare system has been the major cause in the rise of single mothers, they do believe in government-assisted work programs and childcare benefits over welfare as a solution to this dilemma. They found that there is some evidence that children from single parents are less likely to be successful (but neglect to point out this is probably due to poverty, which these authors note is more typical of single-parent families since they have incomes of about 40% of two-parent families). They also found that negative consequences of employed wives are only found in couples with traditional values who find it necessary for the wife to work but who actually believe she should stay at home. The book includes good tables showing comparative poverty rates for single versus two-parent families, numbers of black versus white single-mother families and the increase of all single-parent families since 1940. See McLanahan's earlier article, 166.

Genevie, Louise and Eva Margolies. *The Motherhood Report: How Mothers Feel About Being Mothers.* New York: Macmillan, 1987. See 40 for annotated entry.

156. Gladow, Nancy, and Margaret Ray. "The Impact of Informal Support Systems on the Well Being of Low Income Single Parents." *Family Relations* 35: 1 (1986): 113–123.

This is a study on non-traditional support systems which affect the well-being of low income families headed by women. The authors found that formal support systems such as social workers, counselors and therapists can have positive effects on low income single-parent families. However, less formal support systems, i.e., nuclear families, friends and relatives, should not be overlooked as a source of increasing the well-being of low income single parents and should be used interchangeably with social service support systems. These kinship supports encouraged the women to remain on their own rather than re-enter abusive or dependent relationships, helped them to find work and take care of their children. See Smith (173) for a contrasting viewpoint toward informal support systems.

157. Glubka, Shirley. "Out of the Stream: An Essay on Unconventional Motherhood." *Feminist Studies* 9: 2 (Summer 1983): 223–234.

Glubka writes as a mother who has chosen to give up custody of her child (see Valeska, 250). She became a single mother soon after the birth of her son. After three years Glubka felt that she could not do the kind of work involved in mothering; consequently, she gave up her child to another woman. She points out that it was not the child which she disliked but the work of being a mother and that she never managed to learn the trick of doing two things at once: responding to her child and taking care of herself. Glubka notes that there were two demands which haunted her after giving up her child: one from genuine pain and the other which came from the myth and illusion of the institution of motherhood. Glubka states that she is a feminist and that her feminism gave her the support to live with her decision. It is interesting to look at this statement in relation to Gerson's article "Feminism and the Wish for a Child" (42) wherein she correlates a negative relationship between feminism and the motivation for parenthood. Glubka points out that hundreds of children in the U.S. alone are murdered each year by their parents, yet she still lives "in the closet" in relation to giving up her child due to the adverse reactions of many people. See Mack's response to this article, 164.

158. Hopkinson, Angela. *Single Mothers: The First Year.* Edinburgh: Scottish Council for Single Parents, 1976.

Hopkinson focuses on poor Scottish mothers who have few choices in their first years as single mothers. She looks at the effects of housing, employment opportunities and support networks on these women and offers positive and realistic suggestions for change including accessible day-care and job training. This small study is important in its documentation of the social and financial problems encountered by single mothers and can be useful for showing the universality of the problems faced by impoverished single mothers regardless of race or nationality. See Kamerman (159) for a U.S. equivalent to this study.

159. Kamerman, Shelia B. and Alfred J. Kahn. *Mothers Alone: Strategies For a Time of Change.* Dover: Mass.: Auburn House, 1988.

Kamerman looks primarily at the situation of single mothers in the United States who are dependent on government assistance. She examines their economic problems and the various agencies that are available to help them. The book includes many tables and statistics and is a good source of the economic facts relating to single mothers. Kamerman briefly examines what other countries besides the United States are doing to assist single parents and makes suggestions as to what changes could be made within our present system. This book is a good companion to Hopkinson's study, 158. See also Kamerman's earlier book on working mothers.

160. Keith, Pat, and Robert Schafer. "Correlates of Depression Among Single-Parent Employed Women." *Journal of Divorce* 5: 3 (1982): 49–59.

Fifty-two single-parent women were examined for depression. It was found that those with non-traditional orientations were less likely to suffer from depression as the result of spending more time at work which they enjoyed. Women who had expected to remain housewives were consequently likely to be in unsatisfactory jobs and therefore, were generally not happy about working. Sex-role orientation rather than economic placement appeared to be the predictor for depression.

161. Klein, Carole. *The Single Parent Experience*. New York: Walker, 1973.

Addressed to single parents who have chosen this role, Klein believes these women (and men) have unique problems in society because their choice calls traditional values into question. Klein points out the term "family" can have a very different meaning for a single parent, taking in a much wider range of people while at the same time, society views single mothers as just that: not parents, not a family. Many of the parents who speak here note that being a parent is not, as society would have us believe, dependent upon marriage. The consensus regarding the psychological effects of single parenting on the child are negligible although it was found that single parents tend to be somewhat overprotective (see Kornfein et al., 162). It is the parents' attitudes toward being single which is more important than the experience of single parenting itself (which correlates to the attitudes of working mothers toward their work, see Barnett, 180). See also Merrit (168) and Renvoize (169) for similar studies.

162. Kornfein, Madeleine, Thomas Weisner et al. "Comparative Socialization Practices in Traditional and Alternative Families" in Michael E. Lamb, ed. *Nontraditional Families: Parenting and Child Development*. Hillsdale, N.J.: Lawrence Erlbaum, 1982, pp. 315–346.

The authors found three types of single mothers: "The Nest Builder" who planned to have a child, who were the oldest, more career-oriented and most socially, economically and psychologically sufficient; "The Post Hoc Adapters" who didn't intend to become pregnant but were happy once they were, who were more dependent on networks of friends and relatives with which to share housing and childcare and were usually less educated and had lower-level jobs; "The Unwed Mothers" were the least happy, youngest, had the lowest level jobs and were usually totally dependent on others for their survival. Even though a single mother's behavior in having a child on her own indicates unconventional attitudes, the authors found that the nest builders scored highest on sex-egalitarian values while the unwed mothers were quite traditional. Other findings include: only women with high occupational statuses worked while their children were infants and after three years 51% of the single mothers in this study were still not working. However single mothers as a whole are more likely than other mothers to work full-time when they do work. The authors found that single mothers showed a preference for girl children at birth and that their childrearing was distinctive in a conscious desire not to sex-stereotype their children. The authors point out that although single mothers tend to take their children to doctors for behavioral or psychological problems (see Klein, 161), this may be due to the single mothers' lack of support within the household and related to the fact that 42% of these mothers express ambivalence about their lifestyle. See 57 for another essay by these authors.

163. Kriesberg, Louis. *Mothers in Poverty: A Study of Fatherless Families*. Chicago: Aldine Publishing, Co., 1970.

Kriesberg's study focuses on single mothers with young children living in low-income public housing. He sees the poverty of these women as related to their roles in society, as wives and mothers, financially dependent on men so that when marriages are dissolved by divorce, desertion or death, the women often face economic disaster. His early enlightened views noted that if women were raised to expect to hold jobs and consequently educated for employment, had equal job opportunities, pay and good childcare, this economic dependency and subsequent threat of poverty would be removed. Kriesberg also looks at the well-being of children and marital stability in relation to working mothers and concludes that there is no negative correlation.

Lynn, David Brandon. *Daughters and Parents: Past, Present and Future*. Monterey, Calif.: Brooks/Cole, 1979. See 119 for annotated entry.

164. Mack, Phyllis. A Response to Shirley Glubka's "Out of the Stream: An Essay on Unconventional Motherhood" (157). *Feminist Studies* 10: 1 (Summer 1984): 141–149.

Mack's response to Glubka's article is from a single mother by choice who is sympathetic to another woman's need to give up her child. She feels that voluntary single parenting is a radical decision because it questions the value of the nuclear family. But she also believes that a "feminist perspective on motherhood should do more than shatter myths about maternal instinct and the sanctity of the patriarchal family." She feels that there is a new feminist attitude of anti-mothering (which concurs with Gerson's findings, see 42) whereas there is much about mothering that is positive and should be applauded.

165. Mason, Mary Anne. *The Equality Trap*. New York: Simon & Schuster, 1988.

Like Weitzman (176), Mason looks at the effects of no-fault divorce on women, the most obvious being a lowering of their standard of living, the necessity for paid employment outside the home and the need for childcare for women with children. She feels that a family with children is seldom an egalitarian arrangement but rather functions as a mutual-support society. When such a family breaks up, few women are able to maintain the costs or care of their children, much less their own, without help from the fathers and their own employers, which is seldom forthcoming. Mason argues against equality in the workplace because a totally egalitarian ideal neglects the special considerations which mothers need: children's sick leave, flexible hours, part-time work with medical benefits, childcare assistance. She feels that the concept of equal pay for equal work is used against women with children. Her solutions focus on making the work situation complement the home situation and acceptance of the fact that most women will work outside the home in the future and that many will bear and be responsible for the children.

166. McLanahan, Sara. "Family Structure and Stress: A Longitudinal Comparison of Two-Parent and Female-Headed Households." *Journal of Marriage and the Family* 45: 2 (1983): 347–357.

This study concludes that female heads of families do experience more stress than their married counterparts, which is hardly a surprise. But it is the effects of marriage disruption and dissolution rather than the experience of single parenting that contributes to the women's stress related experiences. An earlier article by McLanahan (*Journal of Marriage and the Family* 43: 3 (1981): 600–612) found that women attempting to establish a new identity post-divorce prospered from loose-knit networks with friends and relatives while those attempting to maintain their existing identities needed close-knit networks for their well-being.

167. Mendes, Helen. "Single-Parent Families: A Typology of Life Styles." *Social Work* 24: 3 (1979): 193–202.

Mendes examines different types of families, including the "executive parent" who takes care of everything and encounters a great deal of stress. She looks at the pros and cons of each situation and concludes that there is as much variety in single-parent families as there is in the traditional dual-parent family and that there are different stress factors for each type of family. The sole executive is a single parental figure actively involved in a child's life who often suffers from the tyranny of the two-parent family model. In contrast, an auxiliary parent shares one or more parental responsibilities with a non-live-in parent figure. Other single family types include unrelated and related substitutes.

168. Merritt, Sharyne, and Linda Steiner. *And Baby Makes Two: Motherhood without Marriage*. New York: Franklin Watts, 1984.

This book is based on a nationwide study of just over 100 single women who chose to become single mothers either through birth or adoption between the ages of 28 and 42 (see Renvoize, 169 and Klein, 161 for similar studies). These women were primarily white, middle-class and college educated who came from intact homes. The authors' focus is on the women's decisions, experiences and feelings; the women speak for themselves throughout the book. They all concur that finances should be a priority in deciding to have a child and that their social lives changed in unexpected ways: men were still available but time and interest were not. The authors believe that if nothing else, a father has symbolic value in our two-parent culture. However, they also feel that single parents who choose to have children can ultimately be successful. An appendix includes the legal aspects of single-parenting as they pertain to custody, child support, etc.

Price, Jane. *Motherhood: What It Does To Your Mind*. London: Pandora Press, 1988. See 74 for annotated entry.

169. Renvoize, Jean. *Going Solo: Single Mothers by Choice*. Boston: Routledge & K. Paul, 1985.

Going Solo deals with why women choose to be single mothers, as opposed to becoming single mothers by default. It gives examples of how they go about becoming pregnant and looks at both the problems and the positive aspects of single mothering by choice. The book has only a small section dealing with the effect on the children of these single mothers as most of the children were still quite young at the time of the study. Renvoize offers a positive view of single mothering, but it should be pointed out that the mothers are mainly middle- and upper-middle-class British and American white women who can afford to make this choice. See Merritt and Steiner (168) and Klein (161) for other books on single motherhood by choice.

170. Richard, Jill V. "Addressing Stress Factors in Single-Parent Women-Headed Households." *Women & Therapy* 1 (Fall 1982): 15–27.

This article begins by addressing the definition of the term "single-parent mother," noting that in the past this group of women has been defined in a negative manner: "divorced," "widowed" or "unwed mothers." The article points to the socio-economic inequalities that single-parent mothers are made to endure. It notes that these problems are different from those encountered by male single parents. In addition, stress, which is high among single-parent mothers, is due, in part, to discriminatory social policies, such as housing and childcare, biased employment policies and limitations on community services, which are all too often tailored to two-parent families needs.

171. Ross, Heather L., and Isabel Sawhill. *Time of Transition: The Growth of Families Headed by Women.* Washington, D.C.: Urban Institute, 1975.

A statistical report which shows the growing trend of families headed by women. One section includes black families; another is on welfare and children. There are numerous tables and appendices and each chapter has its own bibliography. Although technical to read, it offers insights into the facts of single-parent families, including the high incidence of lack of child support and lowered standards of living.

172. Salpin, Beverly. *The Magic Washing Machine: A Diary of Single Motherhood.* Mesquite, Tex.: Ide House, 1983.

Written as a journal, Salpin records the tribulations and a few joys of being a working-class single mother by choice. An opening letter to her son at six years and a closing letter to her mother form the framework for Salpin's journal, which is poignantly written.

173. Smith, Michael. "The Social Consequences of Single Parenthood: A Longitudinal Perspective." *Family Relations* 29: 1 (1980): 75–81.

Smith has found that loneliness and a lack of support networks are the major problems for single parents. Unlike Gladow and Ray (156), Smith believes that "natural" support systems such as family and friends often do not offer enough help to the single parent. He concludes, as do Bilge and Kaufman (146) and Brown et al. (150), that good networking systems are an absolute necessity to the success of single-parent families.

Wearing, Betsy. *The Ideology of Motherhood: A Study of Sydney Suburban Mothers.* Boston: Allen and Unwin, 1984. See 87 for annotated entry.

174. Weiss, Robert Stuart. *Going it Alone: The Family Life and Social Situation of the Single Parent.* New York: Basic Books, 1979.

This is a supportive study of the single parent, particularly single mothers who constitute the majority of single parents. Weiss bases his theories on interviews with single parents and concentrates on the inequities within the present day social system which make the lives of single parents particularly difficult. He also studies the effects of single parenting on children. Written from a feminist viewpoint, this book is still the major work today on single parenting. It is not based solely on statistics and economic facts, as is much of Kamerman's (159) work, but also on personal encounters.

175. Weiss, Robert. "Growing Up a Little Faster: The Experience of Growing Up in a Single-Parent Household." *Journal of Social Issues* 35: 4 (1979): 97–111.

Weiss proposes a theory as to the structure and functioning of the single-parent household. His premise is that the two-parent household maintains a hierarchy that the one-parent household can forego. The consequences for the children are a fostering of early maturity as well as a higher degree of closeness with their parents because of the partnership arrangement. Weiss looks at how this early maturity is formed in the children of single-parent households and concludes that this is not a problem for most children, particularly older ones. Weiss's most startling conclusion is that "the single-parent family, insofar as it requires that the children within it behave responsibly, may, in this respect, be a better setting for growing up than the two-parent family."

176. Weitzman, Lenore J. *The Divorce Revolution: The Unexpected Social and Economic Consequences for Women and Children in America.* New York: The Free Press, 1985.

This book deals with the financial repercussions of no-fault divorce for women in terms of property settlement, alimony and child support and shows how women are unfairly treated in the legal system. Weitzman points out the phenomenon of "relative deprivation" whereby the better off the woman was before the divorce, the worse off she will be after it. Wives from lower-income families have 71% of pre-divorce family income while wives of middle- and high-income families have a much lower percentage, down as far as 29%. In both cases, the men are better off after the divorce. In comparing income to needs, divorced men experience an average of 42% rise in their standards of living in the first year after divorce, while women and children experience a 73% decline. A notable point which Weitzman makes is that men with incomes of $30, 000 to $50, 000 are just as likely to avoid child support as men with incomes under $10, 000.

This book is based on interviews with family court judges and lawyers, divorced men and women as well as an analysis of 2, 500 court dockets. Weitzman not only identifies the problem that "current child support awards are too low, poorly enforced and place a disproportionate financial burden on mothers" but goes on to make recommendations for change. These include changes in property laws, legal support for women and easy access to child support. See Dornbusch and Strober (153) and Mason (165) for other studies on the effects of no-fault divorce.

177. Worell, Judith. "Single Mothers: From Problems to Policies." *Women & Therapy* 7: 4 (1988): 3–14.

This article argues that single motherhood is an issue that should be shared by children and men alike: children because it is their well-being that is to be protected and men because they assume several roles in the lives of the children and mothers directly and indirectly, as co-parents, employers of mothers and mothers' therapists. (This article is tailored to the therapist as are most articles in this publication.) Single motherhood is a community and matrimonial issue, as evidenced by frequently occurring problems of poverty, stigmatization and victimization in the lives of these women. This article urges therapists to get involved in policy issues affecting this part of the population and stresses the importance of making the single-mother family form socially acceptable.

V.

Working Mothers: Good or Bad?

All mothers work. Feminists usually avoid using the term "working mothers" in order to raise consciousness that mothers are working when they are home. Within the limits of this bibliography, however, I sometimes use "working mothers" to refer to mothers who work at paid employment.

It is notable how many studies, including books, journal articles and stories in the popular press, have been written in the past two decades about mothers who work at paid employment. A whole issue of *Journal of Marriage and The Family* (34: 1, 1974) was devoted to the subject. It is evidently an area of family relations which is of concern to a great many people. Two bibliographies have been published on working women: *Women at Work: An Annotated Bibliography* by M.L. Bickner (Los Angeles: University of California, Institute of Industrial Relations, 1974) includes 76 entries under working mothers and *Determinants and Consequences of Maternal Employment: An Annotated Bibliography, 1968–1980* by Marsha Hurst and Ruth Zambrana (Washington, D.C.: Business and Professional Women's Foundation, 1981) includes 198 entries, with sections on popular books and magazines, "how-to" and childrearing books, as well as professional articles and clinical studies.

In general, the consensus regarding the effects of maternal employment is that it benefits both the children and the mother, at least according to Jessie Bernard (9), Anita Shreve (223), Laura Lein (275) and Arlene and Jerome Skolnick (280). What is a detriment for mothers with preschool children is not the fact of their working but the lack of good quality affordable day care. Many recent articles and books which pertain solely to the effects of working mothers on young children are very positive, pointing out that children are more stimulated by spending time with other caretakers and peers in an environment outside of the home. They include those by Cheryl Hayes and Shelia Kamerman (197), Lois Hoffman (200), Adel and Allen Gottfried (195) and the Skolnicks. According to these authors, mothers who have a break from full-time childcare are usually more attentive to and patient with their children.

The early, pre-1970 literature on mothers who worked outside the home was primarily concerned with the effects on the children, not on whether it was a positive or negative experience for the mothers (see Hoffman, 199). The only acceptable reason for a mother to be employed outside the home was economic necessity; any other reason was deemed selfish and not in the best interests of the child. Opponents of this position were Ian Nye and Lois Hoffman who in their 1963 book, *The Employed Mother in America* (213), pointed out that there was little difference between children of working and non-working mothers and if anything, children whose mothers worked exhibited higher levels of self-motivation. Hoffman's book and articles written a decade later come to the same conclusions (see 198–200); her contribution to the study of working mothers is notable.

Hoffman has shown how daughters of working mothers, particularly those with careers, are far less traditionally oriented than girls brought up by full-time mothers. Robert Hansen and Mary Chernovetz (196) and D.M. Millet (211) concur. The mothers themselves also benefit from better health and feelings of self-worth. They also usually enjoy their relationships with their children more than do mothers who are at home all day. One of the most important recent findings by Grace Baruch, et al. in their book, *Lifeprints*, is that the highest levels of personal satisfaction are achieved by women who have combined a meaningful career with motherhood (297). Many other articles and books (see Jean Curtis, 189, Rosalind Loring and Herbert Otto, 206, and Paula Pietromonaco et al., 214) also attest to the benefit of multiple roles. Even women who report that they are overworked and overtired still feel that they have made the right choice by working (Bodin and Mitelman, 182 and Curtis, 189). The collections of essays edited by Sara Ruddick and Pamela Daniel (222) and Jayme Curley (188) and written by professional and creative mothers emphasize this point.

A key factor in studying the effects of working mothers on their families and themselves is the mother's attitude toward herself and her work as passed on to her children. Both Shreve and Hayes and Kamerman found that, as with the lack of day care noted above, it is not the working itself which is the issue but the societal, familial and personal attitudes toward the concept of working mothers which can be problematic (see also Rudd and McKenry 221, Price 216, Aldous 261 and Mischel 212).

Many mothers have ambivalent feelings about working outside the home, which is hardly surprising. These feelings are only exacerbated by the additional strains of negative attitudes in society. The primary problem for these working mothers is too much work, since it is a universal fact (Cook, 186) that the majority of women, even if they hold full-time jobs outside their homes, are responsible for the children and the household, including the major tasks of cleaning and cooking. Alice Cook found that even in communist countries where more day care is provided since women are expected to work at paid employment, women are still doing most of the labor at home as well.

Curtis's research found that women are also considered to be the psychological parent, even if they are in a shared parenting situation. Joseph Pleck (215) picks up on this theme and looks at men's attitudes toward an equal division of home labor between dual working parents. His findings are disheartening.

Carolyn Adams and Kathryn Winston in researching *Mothers at Work* (178) found that women are limited in their careers as a result of their family roles while Nickie Fonda and Peter Moss in *Mothers in Employment* (191) found that just women's anticipation of the mothering role at some point in their life kept them from pushing their careers further along. Career versus job is just one variable, although a key one, which must be taken into consideration when studying mothers who work for pay. Mothers with careers that they have chosen have very different attitudes toward their working than do mothers who must work at less satisfying jobs. These variables are compounded by race, education, age and sex of children, marital status and social class. One of the most interesting findings is that children of working class parents often want to work rather than continue with their education, even if the parents had planned for them to go on to college (see Curtis, 189).

Women who both mother and work at paid employment are pioneers. Most of their own mothers did not work outside the home, at least while their children were young. It is a big step both for mothers and the childcare experts to get beyond the idea that a full-time mother is a necessity for the well-being of her child.

BIBLIOGRAPHY—
WORKING MOTHERS

178. Adams, Carolyn Teich, and Kathryn Teich Winston. *Mothers at Work. Public Policies in the United States, Sweden, and China.* New York and London: Longman, 1980.

This study looks at career limitations which women face due to their familial roles. In the U.S. women leave their work for periods of time, seek part-time work and actually experience downward mobility in their jobs. The authors compare women's experience in the United States to Scandinavia and China where middle-class opinion in one and party doctrine in the other stress the superior value of work outside the home. In both countries government social programs offer support services and benefits which assist women in their family roles, thereby benefiting the whole of society. The authors describe the three governments' programs of family planning, maternity benefits, childcare, home help and welfare assistance to single-parent families. Next, they look at the factors accounting for these policies such as women's own efforts to improve their economic status and the prevailing beliefs in the three political cultures regarding the relationship between families and government. The United States falls far behind the other two in terms of governmental responsibility for families due to a policy of non-interference. This is an interesting fact as the people who advocate less government intervention in family affairs are usually the same ones who want the government to regulate women's reproductive lives.

179. Apter, Terri. *Why Women Don't Have Wives: Professional Success in Motherhood.* New York: Schocken Books, 1985.

Apter begins from the vantage point that while many things to do with women have changed, i.e., job opportunities and financial independence, motherhood with its demands and needs has remained the same. He looks at how women have begun to take part in the working world while continuing to be mothers and he points out that although these women are exceptions, they exhibit a new pattern. (Statistically Apter is incorrect in assuming that these women are exceptional when in fact they are the majority.) According to Apter his own mother was a superwoman, which he sees as an indication of a feminine weakness because this lifestyle is based on the belief that women must be better than men. Like Cardozo (185), Apter believes women should separate their childrearing and professional aspirations into separate time periods. He concludes that the majority of young women today intend to work and pursue careers for most of their period of time. This book offers a mixed message to women: while promoting the concept of work and careers as being valid pursuits for women, parenting and child-raising is still assumed to be the desire of and a necessity for women.

180. Barnett, Rosalind C. "Multiple Roles and Well-Being: A Study of Mothers of Preschool Age Children." *Psychology of Women Quarterly* 7: 2 (Winter 1982): 175–178.

Barnett examines the relation of well-being to involvement in multiple roles through a study of a 134 white women. All of the subjects were in intact marriages and the mothers of a least one pre-school child. The indicators of well-being which were used were: self-esteem and satisfaction with current role patterns. In contrast to Hoffman (199) and to her own findings published a year later (297), Barnett found no differences in levels of well-being between employed and non-employed women. However, the stronger the commitment to work among employed women, the higher their well-being, correlating with Hoffman's findings. A longer paper with the same title can be found in the Schlesinger Library working papers. It should be noted that earlier (pre-1970) studies on multiple roles showed a negative correlation to the well-being of working mothers. The numerous articles which have appeared in recent years on this subject point to the opposite conclusions. See also Waldron and Jacobs (226) and Pietromonaco et al. (214) for other studies. A later study by Barnett written with Grace Baruch, "Role Quality, Multiple Role Involvement, and Psychological Well-Being in Midlife Women" in the *Journal of Personality and Social Psychology* 51 (1986), proposes that because each person has limited time and energy, women with multiple roles often experience role overload and role conflict. According to Bodin and Mitelman (182) and Curtis (189), this does not pose a problem. See 314 for another article by Barnett and Baruch, as well as *Spouse, Parent, Worker: On Gender and Multiple Roles* edited by Faye Crosby (New Haven: Yale University, 1987), which contains two pieces by these authors.

Beckett, Joyce O. "Working Wives: A Racial Comparison." *Social Work* (November 1976): 463–471. See 253 for annotated entry.

181. Berg, Barbara. *The Crisis of the Working Mother: Resolving the Conflict Between Family and Work*. New York: Summit Books, 1986.

Berg, a mother of two young children, has based her research on a series of interviews and questionnaires with working mothers as well as the writing of a variety of psychologists and sociologists. She looks at the differences between women today who are choosing dual roles of careers and mothering and these women's own mothers, most of whom were full-time home makers. She found that many women, even though their lives were studies of strength and achievement, had a fragmented self-image. Berg looks at the pioneering experience of working mothers today who do not have models in their own mothers yet who hope to be the models for their own children. She feels we must work to integrate the values we have taken from our mother with those we have found since leaving her. Berg attributes our ambivalent feelings toward leaving our children for work as stemming from guilt at leaving, at least symbolically, our own mothers behind in order to lead a different life. Berg points out that if we can see how we have incorporated certain things from our mothers, particularly our love and commitment to our children, we will be less ambivalent in our chosen dual-role of working mother.

182. Bodin, Jeanne, and Bonnie Mitelman. *Mothers Who Work: Strategies for Coping*. New York: Ballantine Books, 1983.

The authors state that "we use the term working mother and professional to refer to women who are generating income, even though we know that all mothers work inside the home as homemakers and nurturers" (p. 3). Their focus is on the impact on family life of mothers who work for economic reasons and how these mothers cope with their dual commitments. The authors received many letters from working mothers during their writing of this book and over one half of it consists of chapters written by other women with subjects including "Corporate Career and a Baby," "Venturing Forth at Forty," "Single Mother" and "Shared Parenting." The parts written by the two authors look at why women work and strategies for coping. They found that most women feel good about themselves and their roles and see themselves as providers as well as nurturers, at the same time as they experience stress and conflict; a lack of time was noted as the primary pressure. The most noteworthy finding was that regardless of the stress encountered, these mothers had no ambivalence regarding the positive effect of working mothers on families (see Curtis, 189 for similar findings).

183. Borman, Kathryn, Daisy Quarm and Sarah Gideonse. *Women in the Workplace: Effects on Families*. Norwood, N.J.: Ablex, 1984.

This book is concerned with the consequences of women's participation in the labor force on childcare arrangements, family roles and government policy. In her introduction Gideonse shows how governments are hampered by ideologies and mythologies concerning the family and women's role in it. The remainder of the book is divided into three sections: the first examines the effect of maternal employment on children's development and subsequent socialization as adults. Most of the articles include reviews of current research which is useful for a more in-depth study.

184. Bruce, John A. "The Role of Mothers in The Social Placement of Daughters: Marriage or Work ?" *Journal of Marriage and the Family* 33: 3 (August 1974): 492–497.

Although planned marriages are not the norm in the United States, it has been found that mothers are often involved in their daughter's courtship. Maternal employment and the probability that the daughter will also be involved in work reduce "launching" behavior in mothers (see Hansen, 196 and Hoffman, 199 for similar findings). A career is more prominent than a mate in the minds of working mothers.

185. Cardozo, Arlene. *Sequencing*. New York: Athenaeum, 1986.

Cardozo defines sequencing as a combination of modern feminism with traditional mothering whereby a women first has a full-time, fulfilling career, then takes time out to concentrate her energies (as if they are all needed) on being a full-time mother and, finally, idyllically reintegrates her professional life into her home life. See Apter (179) for the same idea. Cardozo believes that women cannot have a full-time career and close family relationships at the same time. She has based this book on interviews with 350 women in various stages including some "super" women who are combining careers and motherhood; (her introduction is titled "The Death of Superwomen"). The problem with Cardozo's theory is that it reinforces traditional patterns of behavior. She neglects to point out that full-time mothering and careers as opposed to work are options of few women. Good careers, which are hard enough to come by, seldom allow for leaving and re-entry. Questions left unanswered by Cardozo include why a mother must suffer the stress of a child being sick as opposed to a father, i.e., the mother takes off work, not the father, and why women, as opposed to men, are meant to give up their work for full-time parenting. It is notable that Cardozo's bibliography includes many popular culture references.

186. Cook, Alice H. *The Working Mother: A Survey of Problems and Programs in Nine Countries.* Ithaca, N.Y.: New York State School of Industrial and Labor Relations, 1975.

The author visited nine countries (Sweden, Israel, East and West Germany, Romania, Austria, Russia, Japan and Australia) in order to study the working conditions of employed mothers and national policies which either encouraged or discouraged their working. The author herself had been a single working mother and felt that working mothers epitomized the problems of women in general, i.e., outside work and household responsibilities. A universal finding, in communist and non-communist countries alike, was that working women are also responsible for home and childcare, thereby carrying a double burden. One difference that Cook found was that in communist nations women are expected to work; therefore, social policies allow for day care needs. But even in these countries the women still are responsible for maintaining the home. Cook advocates immediate provisions for childcare and part-time work until society equalizes parenting roles. In Scandinavia, where parental equality is the most advanced, most nurturing duties still fall to the mother.

187. Cook, Barbara Ensor. *A Mother's Choice: To Work or Not While Raising a Family.* White Hall, Va.: Betterway Publications, 1988.

The book's title belies its specific, if unmentioned, audience: women who can choose whether or not to work outside the home. While financial motivations are well examined, Cook is clearly not addressing women who must work to survive. Aided by interviews which she conducted, Cook discusses personal and family pressures involved in this decision, as well as those that come from friends, colleagues and society at large. The pros and cons to be weighed are portrayed in all their complexity as are the work options themselves. The author stresses the importance of women's ability to control their own lives and seems to have no hidden agenda on the issue of work outside the home.

188. Curley, Jayme, et al. *The Balancing Act II*. Chicago: Chicago Review Press, 1981.

The Balancing Act: A Career and a Baby (Chicago: Swallow Press, 1976) written six years before by the same authors looked at the assumptions, expectations and impact of first children on the lives of women seriously involved in developing careers. This second book includes their original essays as well as an account of each of their experiences over six years of combining parenthood and careers. The five professional women, now in their mid-thirties, include a ceramist, designer, editor, teacher and attorney. They presently have between two and four children. These are white, middle-class, well-educated, financially stable women with supportive husbands, all with flexible schedules and paid childcare allowing them to be equally involved with their children and careers. Although privileged, they address the same situation of many women who are committed to combining these dual roles for the best of all. They conclude that the balancing act is possible. All of these women advanced in their careers and felt strongly enough about the benefits of motherhood to have additional children. They note that childcare is their biggest problem. Some tried sharing the responsibility for children with their husbands but found that the realities of equal parenting were difficult to realize.

189. Curtis, Jean. *Working Mothers*. Garden City, N.Y.: Doubleday, 1976.

This book is based on interviews with over 200 women, men and children. It asks the questions, should a mother work, and if she does, how does it affect both her and her family. Curtis looks at the stress and anxiety related to social change as does Pleck (215). All the women interviewed were overworked and overtired yet the majority said they would not change their lives and felt that they were better off having a variety of activities in their lives (see Bodin and Mitelman, 182). A common fantasy was for unscheduled time to be alone. It is interesting to note that the husbands never expressed a similar need. The women felt that they still developed close ties with their children even though most had gone back to work right after childbirth. This book offers many interesting insights. One which relates to the work of Gilligan (324) is that the mothers are never alone because they see themselves as the "psychological parent" meaning that even if childrearing and household tasks are shared, it is the mother who is most concerned with the day to day life of the child.

190. Feinstein, Karen W. *Working Women and Families*. Volume 4. Sage Yearbooks and Women's Policy Studies. Beverly Hills, Calif.: Sage Publications, 1979.

This book contains thirteen essays on various aspects pertaining to women and work, including blue-collar women, the feminization of poverty, historical trends, house-husbands and job-sharing couples. Many chapters are reprinted from volume 11, numbers one and two of *The Urban and Social Change Review*, special issue on "Women and Work" (April 1978). "Non-Traditional Work Schedules for Women" by Denise Polit points out that the desire of more women to combine mothering and careers or just work outside of the home shows a desire to balance the benefits of family life with personal growth. Unfortunately, society is just barely begining to accommodate these workers with flex-time schedules, day care assistance and reasonable wages.

191. Fonda, Nickie, and Peter Moss, eds. *Mothers in Employment*. Uxbridge: Burnell University Management Programme and Thomas Coram Research Unit, University of London, 1976.

The authors have edited papers from a conference held at Burnell University in 1976. The primary issue which was addressed was the well-being of employed mothers as a crucial factor for both the women and the children. One of the better papers, "Women, Work, and Conflict," is by Susan Ginsberg. One of her findings was that while being a full-time mother with small children may be a transient phase, it determines a woman's whole life in terms of her employment opportunities and her own concept of self-worth. The anticipation of motherhood keeps many women from pursuing advanced education and training. Another paper "The Employer's Attitude to Working Mothers" concludes that managers make decisions based on economic priorities and suggests that a considerable shift in attitude is necessary to accommodate working mothers. Others papers are concerned with child care and economic issues specific to Britain.

192. Frankel, Judith, Mary Anne Minque and Michelle Palude. "The Employed Mother: A New Social Norm." *International Journal of Women's Studies* 5 (May-June 1982): 274–281.

Based on a sample of 238 middle- to upper-class white women, the authors found that the majority of mothers of school age children believed paid employment to be the appropriate choice, indicating that there has been a radical reversal in normative expectations for women.

Genevie, Louise, and Eva Margolies. *The Motherhood Report: How Mothers Feel About Being Mothers.* New York: Macmillan, 1987. See 40 for annotated entry.

193. Gerson, Kathleen. *Hard Choices: How Women Decide about Work, Career, and Motherhood.* Berkeley: University of California, 1985.

Gerson is dissatisfied with prevailing theories of gender and believes that within the patriarchal context women *do* shape their own lives. Two of her assumptions are: there are large social and psychological differences among women, maybe as large as between women and men (see Eisenstein and Jardine, 303); and neither men nor women should be judged to have better characteristics (see Gilligan, 324). Gerson's analysis is based on in-depth interviews with domestic and non-domestic women from a variety of social and economic backgrounds. Gerson found that domestic and non-domestic women denigrated each other's choices, creating deep ideological divisions. She brings up an interesting point, that when feminist women choose not to bear children they are often in agreement with traditionalists that one can not do both, i.e., have a career and be a mother. Gerson defines "reluctant motherhood" as the realization that while children will interfere with careers, childlessness would be worse.

194. Giraldo, Zaida Irene. *Public Policy and the Family: Wives and Mothers in the Labor Force.* Lexington, Mass.: Lexington Books, 1980.

Although this book's primary focus is on the effects of public policy on the family, including tax reforms and the E.R.A, it includes two chapters on working mothers: "Employed Wives and Mothers: Labor-Force Participation" and "Women as Wage-Earners," as well as about 50 tables which compile an array of interesting comparables such as: daily hours of housework by hours of employment and by sex, day care hours and convenience by family type, childcare arrangements, etc. Like other researchers (see Gottfried, 195), the author concludes the government policies must be updated to incorporate the "new" families of single and dual-earner parents.

195. Gottfried, Adel E., and Allen W. Gottfried, eds. *Maternal Employment and Children's Development: Longitudinal Research.* New York: Plenum Press, 1988.

This book includes a foreword by Lois W. Hoffman (see 198–200) who applauds the book for its new insights and its longitudinal data, the first to be compiled on the effects of maternal employment. Mothers' employment status, the hours of weekly employment, part- versus full-time, occupational status and attitudes toward work are all examined for their impact on a variety of children's developmental outcomes. Many hypotheses and a few conclusions are reached, including the fact that maternal employment is not only a gender issue but one affecting the family, workplace and society at large and that the workplace must respond to family issues by creating more family-oriented policies. The Gottfrieds conclude that employment status is non-significant on children's development through the school entry years and is significantly and positively related to educational attitudes of five- to seven-year-olds as well as to father involvement at this same stage. Mothers of higher occupational levels with favorable perceptions of dual-roles had more well-developed children. The Gottfrieds point out that there is a need to distinguish between the mothers' working and unsatisfactory work conditions and childcare arrangements being responsible for child-related problems.

196. Hansen, Robert O., Mary E. Chernovetz and Warren H. Jones. "Maternal Employment and Androgyny." *Psychology of Women Quarterly* 2: 1 (Fall 1977): 76–78.

This article looks at the research reviewed by Hoffman (200) and goes on to study the correlation of androgyny (defined as the identification with desirable masculine and feminine characteristics) in college-aged daughters of working mothers. The result is that employed mothers, being less traditional in their sex roles, help to develop androgynous self-concepts in their daughters. See Lynn (119) for another study on adrogyny.

Harrison, Algea Othella, and JoAnne Holbert Minor. "Interole Conflict, Coping Strategies, and Role Satisfaction Among Single and Married Employed Mothers." *Psychology of Women Quarterly* 6: 3 (Spring 1982): 354–360. See 256 for annotated entry.

197. Hayes, Cheryl D., and Shelia B. Kamerman, eds. *Children of Working Parents: Experiences and Outcomes*. Panel on Work, Family, and Community, Committee on Child Development Research and Public Policy, Commission on Behavioral and Social Sciences and Education, National Research Panel. Washington, D.C.: National Academy Press, 1983.

The consensus of the various authors is that parental employment is not a uniform condition with consistent effects on all children, as compared to factors such as income, race and supportive services. "The Effects of Mothers' Employment on Adolescent and Early Adult Outcomes of Young Men and Women" by Ronald D'Amico et al. includes a review of the extensive literature on the effects of mothers' work on children. These authors found that mothers who are happy with their jobs have better relationships with their children and serve as positive role models as opposed to mothers who are unhappy in their work or domestic role. They also found a strong tendency for mothers to transmit intergenerational behaviors to children, including non-traditional values and career orientations to daughters (see Kohler, 56, for similar findings).

198. Hoffman, Lois W. "The Effects of Maternal Employment on The Child: A Review of the Research." *Developmental Psychology* 10: 2 (1974): 204–228.

The employed mother is viewed as presenting a less traditional sex-role model for her daughters, which in turn results in the daughters having less stereotyped views of male and female roles. This implies not a movement from femininity to masculinity but, as some researchers have stated, to a position of psychological freedom from traditional sex-role constraints on self-concept (see Hansen and Chernovetz, 196).

199. Hoffman, Lois W. "The Professional Woman as Mother" in Ruth B. Kundsin, ed. *Women & Success. The Anatomy of Achievement*. New York: William Morrow, 1974, pp. 222–228.

Hoffman examines the effects of a career on mothering, of mothering on a career and the effects of combining these two roles on women's personal satisfactions. Although it is evident that most careers are slowed down as a result of the career woman's becoming a mother, many recent studies have shown that the combination of career and motherhood results in the highest level of personal satisfaction (see Roland 220, Shreve 223 and Baruch et al. 297). The author primarily focuses on the effects of a mother's professional status on her child (see Hoffman's earlier study with Ian Nye, 213). The majority of studies reveal a positive effect, especially for daughters, who do not assume that women are less competent than men. Women with higher achievement aspirations are most likely to be the daughters of educated, professional women.

200. Hoffman, Lois W., and F. Ivan Nye, eds. *Working Mothers*. New York: Jossey-Bass, 1974.

The aim of these authors was to compile research findings on the effects of maternal employment on the family from the fields of psychology and sociology and to summarize them in non-technical language. They found that physical and emotional health appeared to be better for working mothers than for non-working mothers. Working mothers of three or fewer children seemed to enjoy their relationships with their children more than did non-working mothers. They conclude that maternal employment is neither bad nor good in itself, but rather it has specific effects under specific conditions (see Hayes and Kamerman, 197 for similar findings and Rollins, 124 for contrasting ones). They also point out that full-time employment and full responsibility for childcare and housekeeping is too much work for the mother, creating a variety of problems. The book includes a thorough, although early (pre-1970), bibliography on working mothers.

201. Howell, Mary C. "The Effects of Maternal Employment on the Child." *Pediatrics* 52: 3 September 1973.

This article points out that the bias against working mothers is so rampant that questionnaires are phrased so that the responses will be negative. Very few studies had been done prior to 1973 to demonstrate the positive effects of working mothers.

202. Huston-Stein, A., and A. Higgins Trenk. "Development of Females from Childhood thru Adulthood: Careers and Feminine Role Orientations" in Paul Baltes, ed. *Life Span Development and Behavior*. Volume 1. New York: Academic Press, 1978.

This study of women's roles within the family and workplace examines historical changes, sociocultural factors, men's and women's attitudes toward women's roles and childhood influences on later developmental patterns. Like Hansen and Chernovetz (196), these authors found that early socialization into non-traditional behaviors resulted in higher standards of achievement for women. Although the majority of women since 1950 have changed their focus to include both family and work, few have obtained high status or salary from their work due to both internalized beliefs concerning their own competence and external discrimination. In terms of women, the authors found that employed middle-class white mothers have the highest levels of life satisfaction and that problems stem from role overload, rather than role conflict. This is similar to Hoffman's findings (198).

203. Jensen, Larry, and Marilyn Borges. "The Effects of Maternal Employment on Adolescent Daughters." *Adolescence* 21 (Fall 1986): 659–666.

This small study seeks to uncover the effects of maternal employment on adolescents. It concluded that the strongest parent-child relationship was between the father and the daughter in families of non-employed mothers. In this family situation the daughters perceived their fathers to be kinder and in better spirits. They also tended to note less stress in the home.

204. Kamerman, Shelia B. *Parenting in an Unresponsive Society: Managing Work and Family Life*. New YorK: Free Press, 1980.

Writing along a similar vein to Michelson (210), Kamerman sees the increasing entry of married women with pre-school children into the labor force as the most significant development in families in recent decades. The focus of this study on working mothers with young children is the implications of this phenomenon on children, families and society in general. Kamerman sees wage earning and parenting carried out simultaneously as characteristic of most adults in the near future regardless of gender. Kamerman studies both black and white suburban women (from Maplewood, New Jersey) who stemmed from different family types and socio-economic levels to see the resulting consequences of how they manage their work and family lives. Her conclusions are that informal, natural support systems are essential for these women, particularly the help of relatives (see Gladow and Ray, 156), and that income needs surrounding maternity leaves and childcare are of major importance. An interesting statistic which Kamerman found was that in husband-wife families, more black than white mothers work while in mother-only families, more white women work. This book includes a small bibliography with many journal articles and U.S. government reports. See Kamerman's later work on single mothers (159).

205. Krogh, Kathryn Miller. "Women's Motives to Achieve and to Nurture in Different Life Stages." *Sex Roles* 12: 1/2 (1985): 75–90.

Krogh investigated the motivations to achieve and nurture in 60 women between 31 and 37 years old, half of whom had children under four and half of whom had children older. "Life stages" refers to the periods of life which are defined by major events, such as one's youngest child entering full-time school. Krogh defined stage one as mothers with pre-schoolers and stage two as mothers with school age children. She found a lessening of importance of achievement motivation during stage one and an increasing of its importance during stage two. Nevertheless, the need to nurture was still ranked as more important than the need to achieve by women in stage two. Women in both life stages attached tremendous importance to their children and their mothering role. Many women expressed surprise at their changes of feelings regarding mothering and work roles and at the intensity of these feelings.

206. Loring, Rosalind, and Herbert Otto, eds. *New Life Options: The Working Women's Resource Book.* New York: McGraw-Hill, 1976.

Although this is more of a self-help than a feminist book, it is consistent with the findings of many authors annotated herein. In the chapter on single parents the authors found that a common characteristic of these families was lower than average income. They offer the idea that divorce is sometimes the beginning of personal and family growth as both a mother and her children clarify their own self-knowledge. In terms of working mothers it was found that dual roles stimulated the psychological well-being of the woman. Working women were not found to be inadequate mothers but rather the support systems, such as childcare, were found to be the major cause of any problems for working mothers.

207. Lubin, Aasta S. *Managing Success: High-Echelon Careers and Motherhood.* New York: Columbia University Press, 1987.

The author studied five mothers in prestigious, well-paid jobs and egalitarian marriages. They were studied as a sub-culture from an ethnographic point of view in order to learn about them from their own point of view. Lubin found that they had dismissed traditional views of marriage and motherhood and that they were all goal-oriented, energetic and optimistic people. She found that besides their own abilities to work hard, these women depended on help from family, colleagues and housekeepers in order to function well. An interesting fact that Lubin notes is that the less differential in income between spouses, the more the husband's participation in home tasks.

208. Mandelbaum, Dorothy R. *Work, Marriage, and Motherhood: The Career Persistence of Female Physicians*. New York: Praeger, 1981.

Mandlebaum addresses the question of why, in this particular group of career-committed women (being licensed physicians) some are more likely than others to persist in their work. Given the unusually narrow group being studied, this book offers a fascinating look at the pressures experienced by women who have a great deal invested in their careers who quit when becoming mothers (the largest reason given for not working). The initial study was done in 1973–1974, the longitudinal study in 1978–1979. Career persistence positively identified with adversity in early childhood, early goal embedding, the establishment of priorities and identity as doctor first. "Non-persisters" who try to do it all (marry, mother, doctor) often withdraw for a time, then continue when family responsibilities ease.

209. McKaughan, Molly. *The Biological Clock: Reconciling Careers and Motherhood in the 1980s*. New York: Doubleday, 1987.

Along the same lines as Fabe and Wikler (35) and Wilk (227), McKaughan looks at the reasons why women delay having children and why many become consumed by the idea late in their childbearing years. McKaughan also found many women undecided whether or not have children. In order to answer these questions she surveyed 1,000 women through a questionnaire published in *Working Women Magazine* (May 1985) and conducted interviews with 100. Issues addressed were career concerns, loudness of the biological clock, reasons for postponing, earlier and current attitudes toward becoming a mother. She found that women of the 1980s were involved in their work yet also felt their private lives were very important. The reasons they gave for delaying childbirth were that avoiding pregnancy is easy today, they had been educated to want a fulfilling life and finding a good job was usually a reality, they see their mother's lives as limited, sex is safe outside of marriage (the issue of AIDS was not raised here) and that careers, rather than family, gave continuity to their lives.

210. Michelson, William M. *From Sun to Sun: Daily Obligations and Community Structure in the Lives of Employed Women and Their Families.* Totowa, N.J.: Rowman & Allanheld, 1985.

In 1950 11.9% of American women with children under six worked outside the home. In 1981 this percentage had risen to 47.8%. This, according to Michelson, is why there is currently so much interest in maternal employment and why it has become a feminist issue. Based on a survey of 544 Metro Toronto families with children which was conducted in 1980 under the auspices of Canada's Ministry of National Health and Welfare, the purpose of this study was to see how maternal employment affects both women and their children and to offer recommendations for policy changes. It includes many useful tables comparing median incomes, hours of employment, hours spent at domestic tasks, time children spend on activities, etc. One of the most fascinating tables compared the number of children's excursions: children of unemployed mothers went on less excursions than those who had mothers working full- or part-time. One chapter is devoted to comparing the lives of single working mothers to their married counterparts and the effects of lesser financial resources or the help of a spouse. Michelson recommends job sharing and flexibility as well as convenient locations for childcare and transportation systems as means of easing the lives of working mothers. See Kamerman (204) for similar conclusions.

211. Millet, D.M. "Effects of Maternal Employment on Sex Role Perception, Interests and Self-Esteem in Girls." *Developmental Psychology* 11 (May 1975): 405–406.

This study presented a series of questions and situations to a group of 17 kindergarten girls whose mothers were employed and a control group of 17 girls whose mothers were homemakers. They found that the daughters of the working mothers had more non-traditional sex-role perceptions. Hoffman (198) and Hansen and Chernovetz (196) came to the same conclusions. Millet's study also found that daughters of working mothers seemed to be more aggressive than daughters of non-working mothers, but that self-esteem at this age was not affected by maternal employment.

212. Mischel, Harriet Nerlove and Robert Fuhr, eds. "Maternal Employment: Its Psychological Effects on Children and Their Families" in Sanford M. Dornbusch and Myra H. Strober, eds. *Feminism, Children, and the New Families.* New York: Guilford, 1988, pp. 191–211.

These authors conclude, as do Hayes and Kamerman (197), that parental attitudes toward women working including the degree of father involvement in childcare have more of an impact on children than does maternal employment. One interesting point made is that working mothers offer positive role models for their daughters more so than for their sons, although both sexes show increased sex-role flexibility.

213. Nye, F. Ian, and Lois W. Hoffman. *The Employed Mother in America.* Chicago: Rand McNally, 1963.

Although this book was done in 1963, it offers some interesting insights. Most of the studies prior to this time attempted to show the disastrous effects to children of working mothers. But Nye and Hoffman, writing from a feminist viewpoint, show how very few differences between children of working and non-working mothers were found. In fact, there were many positive aspects, such as higher motivation levels, for children of working mothers. (See Hoffman's later studies attesting to this finding, 198.) Hoffman also points out that maternal employment is too heterogeneous a variable to study; it must be broken down by class, education, age of children, etc. In one of her studies Hoffman found that mothers who liked their work often felt guilty and as a result were over-indulgent with their children. Therefore, it was not the employment, but the guilt that was a problem. See Nye and Hoffman's later book (200).

214. Pietromonaco, Paula R., Jean Manis and Katherine Frohardt-Lane. "Psychological Consequences of Multiple Roles." *Psychology of Woman Quarterly* 10 (1986): 373–382.

This study on multiple roles (see other studies on this subject by Barnett, 180, and Waldron and Jacobs, 226) is based on a survey taken to explore potential negative and positive consequences of having multiple roles. Perceptions concerning self-esteem, satisfaction with careers, spouses and children and degrees of life stress were noted. The finding indicated that higher self-esteem and greater job satisfaction came from holding more roles but that neither marital nor parental satisfaction was related. The authors conclude that for working women multiple roles probably enhance psychological well-being.

215. Pleck, Joseph H. *Working Wives, Working Husbands*. Beverly Hills, Calif.: Sage Publications, 1985.

Increasing men's family roles can often mean reducing their paid work time for those men who work 12-hour days or who regularly bring work home. Since husbands often earn more than their wives, this poses a problem for families dependent on a certain amount of income who want to share parenting and household tasks. This is a conflict for men, women and society that must be resolved. Pleck found that men often share more of the tasks at home with wives who work at paid employment because both parties have less time. Pleck cites studies which show that men's job roles, not sex roles, keep them from helping at home, yet it still appears that men, even those whose wives work an equal amount outside of the home, do less work at home. Pleck sees the reasons for this as lack of motivation, skills and support by the men's peers and, sometimes, their wives. See the working papers at Schlesinger Library for additional work by Pleck.

216. Price, Jane. *Motherhood: What it Does to Your Mind.* London: Pandora Press, 1988.

See 74 for the primary annotation of this book. Price states that all mothers work. Some choose the 24-hour-day, seven-days-a-week route in exchange for room and board and partial security while others choose to work outside the home. For many other women, there is no choice. An interesting point which Price makes is the negative feelings many women who choose to work outside the home must encounter and what this does to their self-esteem (see various studies cited throughout, particularly Rudd and McKenry 221). However, this probably depends a great deal on the particular environment; in large urban areas working mothers are usually the norm.

217. Propper, A.M. "The Relationship of Maternal Employment to Adolescent Roles, Activities, and Parental Relationships." *Journal of Marriage and the Family* 34 (1972): 417–421.

The author found no difference in perceptions of parental interests, support and closeness between children of working and non-working mothers. One interesting result of this study was that sons of working-class mothers employed outside the home were less likely to choose their fathers as their most admired male. The author concludes that it is probably incorrect to assume maternal employment affects both sexes the same way and that there could also be class differences.

218. Rapoport, Rhona, Robert Rapoport and Ziona Strelitz. *Fathers, Mothers and Society: Towards New Alliances.* New York: Basic Books, 1977.

Women's expectations of fulfillment in caring for families are not met because they have other, separate needs which cannot be fulfilled by motherhood alone. The authors argue for women to be re-integrated into the labor force. They suggest restructuring the work place, recognition of fathers as active parents and domestic workers, the opening of childcare centers and the education of girls for both family and employment roles. The Rapoports have co-authored another book, *Dual-Career Families Re-Examined* (New York: Harper & Row, 1976).

219. Ritchie, Jane. "Child-Rearing Practices and Attitudes of Working and Full-Time Mothers." *Women's Studies International Forum.* 5: 5 (1982): 419–25.

This study, which compares childrearing practices and attitudes between a group of working and full-time mothers of four-year-olds, found little difference between the two groups in terms of childrearing methods. However, significant differences were discovered in the mothers' attitudes; for instance, working mothers found child rearing more pleasurable. They also had better relationships with their children, who were perceived as well adjusted and happy. Working mothers had more self-esteem and were less anxious about their abilities as mothers. One interesting finding was that husbands of working mothers tended to help more with childcare (see Pleck, 215).

220. Roland, Alan, and Barbara Harris. *Career and Motherhood: Struggles for a New Identity.* New York: Human Sciences Press, 1979.

Roland and Harris offer the consensus that women should pursue dual lives of careers and mothering, even though this is not an easy task. The book includes chapters by the two authors as well as a variety of contributors, including Jane Lazarre, 58. It is an insightful work that offers a positive outlook on working mothers. The authors point out that most women must confront either the option of choosing between full-time mothering and working or the fact of their lack of choice in this matter. In either case, the change of identities will cause anxiety. The authors have focused on women with careers as opposed to nine-to-five jobs because a career implies a commitment to one's potential in the work world. This book investigates the practical, theoretical and psychoanalytical aspects of dual identity.

221. Rudd, Nancy M., and Patrick C. McKenry. "Family Influences on the Job Satisfaction of Employed Mothers." *Psychology of Women Quarterly* 10: 4 (1986): 363–372.

The purpose of this study is to explore the relationship between certain variables in the family that might hinder or enhance the job satisfaction of employed mothers. It would appear that family emotional support and positive attitudes are even more important than physical help from family members for the emotional well-being of the working mother. The researchers found that women can experience role overload while still perceiving their husbands and children as supportive of their employment. It has been found that lower job satisfaction is associated with a reduction in satisfaction with other aspects of one's life. The authors mention a study by P.J. Anderisani, "Job Satisfaction Among Working Women" in *Signs* 3 (1978) which found that a husband's attitude toward his wife's employment was a significant factor in overall job satisfaction for both white and black women. See Aldous (261) for similar findings.

222. Ruddick, Sara, and Pamela Daniels, eds. *Working it Out*. New York: Pantheon Books, 1977.

A collection of essays by women who are writers, scholars, scientists and artists. These women have all produced creative works, often separately from the "jobs" which they hold. Many noted feminists are included such as Merriam Schapiro, Alice Walker, Evelyn Fox Keller and Catherine Stimpson. Although not specifically about working mothers, many of the women are also mothers and describe how they have combined two, sometimes three or four, roles (wife, mother, teacher, writer) into one life. Most have found their children to be a source of support and inspiration which goes along with the studies by Baruch (297) which show that talented women who work are the happiest of all.

223. Shreve, Anita. *Remaking Motherhood: How Working Mothers are Shaping our Childrens' Future*. New York: Viking, 1987.

A positive consensus toward working mothers was found by Shreve in her interviews with working and middle-class mothers, fathers and children. She found that working mothers act as positive role models for their daughters and help to give their sons the potential for greater respect for women. She also found that it is not the working per se that affects the child but what the mother conveys about that work that is passed on to the child (see Rudd and McKenry 221, Aldous 261, Hayes and Kamerman

197 and Mischel 212). An interesting discovery was that many working class mothers wanted their children to go to college but the children themselves wanted to work. Shreve points out that Chodorow's theories (19) which state that women's mothering produces sons whose nurturant capacities have been curtailed are dealing with the traditional nuclear family, which is no longer the majority. Shreve includes chapters on mothers and daughters, mothers and sons and single working mothers.

224. Sokoloff, Natalie. *Mother Work and Working Mothers.* New York: Praeger, 1980.

Sokoloff, as Rich (76) and Westkott (131), blames the institution of motherhood as being organized by and for patriarchy, for the oppression of women, not for the benefit of their mothering. She starts off with a historical development of motherhood as an institution from the time of the "family wage" which supposedly gave men enough money to support their families. She then shows a relationship of motherhood to wage labor whereby women are treated as mothers—former, actual, potential—and thereby paid less. Women are learning that unpaid work at home is benefiting the ruling class and that women's work at home and in the marketplace are closely linked.

225. Strober, Myra. "Two-Earner Families" in Sanford M. Dornbusch and Myra Strober, eds. *Feminism, Children, and the New Families.* New York: Guilford, 1988, pp. 161–190.

Strober offers a critical review of the literature on the relations between wives' employment and marriage, childbearing, divorce and marital satisfaction. She found that although women's employment tends to delay marriage it does not result in a decline. She also noted that employed women have fewer children, that there is a possible positive correlation between working women and higher divorce rates and, finally, that higher degrees of marital solidarity are evidenced in dual-earner couples. See also Chapter Four "Wives and Work: A Theory of the Sex-Role Revolution and its consequences" by Kingsley Davis, pp. 67–86.

226. Waldron, Ingrid, and Jerry A. Jacobs. "Effects of Multiple Roles on Women's Health—Evidence from a National Longitudinal Study." *Women & Health* 15: 1 (1989): 3–19.

This study analyzed data from a national sample of middle-aged women in order to assess the health effects of three roles: worker, spouse and parent. It was found that women who held more roles tended to be in better health (see Hoffman and Nye, 200, for the same finding); however, the effect of each specific role varied and was dependent on race and the roles a particular woman held. The authors quote other researchers such as D. Froberg et al. in their article, "Multiple Roles and Women's Mental and Physical Health: What Have We Learned?," and L.M. Verbrugge, "Role Burdens and Physical Health of Women and Men," both in *Women and Health* 11 (1986), who propose that each role brings benefits, such as increased social contacts, personal satisfactions and self-esteem and that therefore multiple roles contribute to better health and greater psychological well-being. From the studies annotated herein as well as numerous other studies which have been done on the effects of multiple roles on women the evidence appears to be somewhat contradictory. It would seem that Waldron and Jacobs's hypotheses, that involvement in each role has both harmful and beneficial effects depending on specific characteristics of the role and the woman, would be the most accurate. They found, for example, that paid work was beneficial for single white women and black women with young children at home but not necessarily for other women. See Pietromonaco et al. (214) and Barnett (180) for other studies.

Wearing, Betsy. *The Ideology of Motherhood: A Study of Sydney Suburban Mothers*. Boston: Allen and Unwin, 1984. See 87 for annotated entry.

227. Wilk, Carole A. *Career Women and Childbearing: A Psychological Analysis of the Decision Process*. New York: Van Nostrand Reinhold, 1986.

Wilk's book focuses on dual-career couples, particularly the women, who are dealing with the decision whether or not to have children (see McKaughan, 209 and Fabe and Wikler, 35). Wilk believes this decision is affected by early developmental processes and outcomes and she provides a psycho-social childbearing decision model. Those women who were found to be ambivalent usually did not identify with their mothers nor were they fully satisfied with either their career or their marital relationships while those women who intended to have children were committed to their careers while still giving priority to relationships. They also identified more with their mothers. The appendices include the professional and personal characteristics of 12 childless dual-career women which are quite revealing.

228. Wortis, Rochelle P. "The Acceptance of the Concept of the Maternal Role by Behavioral Scientitists: Its Effects On Women" (1971) in Signe Hammer, *Women: Body and Culture.* New York: Harper and Row, 1975, pp. 293–317.

Although written in 1971 so that much of the research cited is now out of date, Wortis offers a useful introduction to these early works. Her purpose is to show that the studies which state that the mother is necessary for the development of her children are based on scientifically inadequate assumptions. She is one of the first researchers to look at the mother's feelings as apart from those of the child. She concludes that in order for women to participate equally in the work force, the transitional goal of sharing work at home with their partners must be accomplished first. She also states that consistent care by sensitive adults, not necessarily mothers, is the basis of good child care.

229. Yogev, Sara, and Andrea Vierra. "The State of Motherhood Among Professional Women." *Sex Roles* 9: 3 (1983): 391–396.

This study of faculty women at Northwestern University found a trend toward permanent childlessness among younger professional women. Their rate of childlessness (67%) is much higher than that of older professionals (22%) or younger women in the general population. The authors conclude that younger professional women may not believe that they can successfully combine motherhood with a career. Possible factors contributing to the decline in fertility, the birth rate and family size since the 1970s include increasing education and career opportunities for women and feminist efforts to change social structures since remaining childless challenges the concept of motherhood as central to a woman's identity.

VI.

Lesbian and Black Mothers, Daughters and Sons: Additional Burdens

Only a small sampling of the current literature on lesbian and black mothers has been annotated here because very few studies solely on mothering exist. The researcher can probably find more information on the subject by consulting general books on black culture and the lesbian experience. Joyce Ladner's *Tomorrow's Tomorrow* (Garden City, N.Y.: Doubleday, 1971) is still the best study of motherhood and black female socialization, according to the editors of *Sage*[1] and the bibliography by Valora Washington in her chapter "The Black Mother in the United States" in *The Different Faces of Motherhood* (10) is another good source.

Politics of the Heart (243) includes an extensive list of references and resources relating to lesbian parenting. Adrienne Rich's essay "Compulsory Heterosexuality and Lesbian Existence" published in *Signs* 5:4 (Summer 1980): 631–660, although not specifically concerned with motherhood offers an important critique of contemporary feminist scholarship, including the work of Chodorow and Baker Miller, and the heterosexist assumptions underlying this discourse. An extensive discussion of this essay by Ann Ferguson and others can be found in *Signs* 7:1 (Fall 1981): 158–199.

These two groups have an important aspect in common: both are extremely threatening to the patriarchy, be it individual men or the state. The relationship between the father, mother and child is fundamental to the functioning of patriarchy. The dependency of the child on the mother and the mother on the father ensures male dominance. Lesbian mothers function without the aid of or desire for a father to support their children and the majority of single mothers in this country are at present black (Table F, U.S. Department of Commerce. 1986. Current Population Reports, Series P-20 #411).

The degree to which these black mothers threaten patriarchy can be seen in the infamous Moynihan Report[2] (1965) that stated that the black matriarchal family was the downfall of black men and black family life. Moynihan was unable to see that it was a lack of resources that often caused the dissolution of black families. Having a father in the family may mitigate the effects of father absence on the children but it will not necessarily contribute to the economic well-being of the family. Roy Austin's article (252) on race and father absence refutes Moynihan's claims and they are unlikely to be taken seriously today.

Although all mothers have many things in common, such as concern and responsibility for their children's development, there are apparently significant differences between black and white mothers and daughters. Both Diane Lewis (259) and Gloria Joseph (257) discuss the strong mother-daughter bonds in black families whereby the mother brings up her daughters to be independent women able to survive without the support of men. Joyce Beckett (253) also investigates differences, in this case between black and white working wives.

As noted before, the activity of mothering is too heterogeneous to be studied without reference to issues such as race, class and economics. Black and lesbian mothers both suffer blatant and subtle forms of prejudice not experienced by white middle-class women. This type of discrimination is bound to affect the way in which a mother functions and, therefore, how a child develops. Evelyn Beck (230) and Elizabeth Gibbs (236) look closely at these issues for lesbian mothers. More studies need to be taken on the effects of ostracization on mothers and children. The children of lesbian mothers will have been brought up somewhat outside of patriarchal society and may have more androgynous personalities than are usually found. Like the children of feminist mothers, they may offer hope for change.

Notes

1. Bell-Scott, Patricia, and Beverly Guy-Sheftall. *Sage* 1:2 (Fall 1984).

2. Moynihan, Daniel P. *The Negro Family: The Case or National Action*. Washington, D.C.: U.S. Dept. of Labor (35), 1965.

BIBLIOGRAPHY—
LESBIAN MOTHERS, DAUGHTERS AND SONS

230. Beck, Evelyn Torton. "The Motherhood that Dare Not Speak Its Name." *Women's Studies Quarterly* 11:4 (Winter 1983): 8–11.

According to Beck, The National Gay Task Force estimates that in 1983 there were between 1,500,000 and 2,000,000 lesbian mothers in the U.S. alone. The majority of these women had children within heterosexual marriages although current trends reveal more lesbians choosing to become mothers through adoption and artificial insemination. On the one hand Beck notes that "a lesbian mother is a mother like any other—good, bad, or indifferent" while on the other she emphasizes the multiple burdens these mothers face. Besides the usual stresses related to childbearing, the lesbian mother is often a single mother who is faced with homophobia in the heterosexual world and suspicion from the lesbian community due to her patriarchal ties. She also must deal with the negative image of the lesbian mother in her own mind and possibly within the minds of her children as well. Beck correctly points out that with the exception of Rich (76), the subject of lesbian motherhood has primarily been addressed by lesbian-feminist journals. She goes on to review Hanscombe and Forster's *Rocking the Cradle* (238) and gives a remarkable number of sources on lesbian mothers in books, journals, women's studies publications, annotated bibliographies and films. *Women's Studies Quarterly* is available from P.O. Box 334, Old Westbury, NY 11568. See Beck's essay in *Politics of the Heart* (243).

231. Berzon, B. "Sharing Your Lesbian Identity with Your Children" in Ginny Vida, ed. *Our Right to Love*. Englewood Cliffs, N.J.: Prentice-Hall, 1978, pp. 69–74.

This chapter deals with how the lesbian mother might share her homosexuality with her children. The author makes suggestions on this matter as well as on how to cope in a situation where mothers must defend their mothering (to society at large and often to the lesbian community) and children are asked to defend their mothers. Another chapter in this book, "Lesbian Mothers in Transition" by Mary Stevens (207–210) looks at the changes (politically, socially) taking place that affect the lives of lesbian mothers.

232. Clausen, Jan. "A Flommy Looks at Lesbian Parenting." *Off Our Backs* 16 (August-September 1986): 16–17.

This commentary written in the first person, was prepared for a conference on feminism. This a very personal, although *not* one-sided viewpoint on lesbian co-parenting as told by a non-biological parent. She speaks of nurturing roles and the emotional and material support she derives from her three-person (female) family. Clausen brings up many internal and external (societal) conflicts that she feels are a result of her chosen situation. One of these is her ambivalence about whether she, herself, wants to have a child. Another is her feeling of being an "outsider," as many lesbian/feminists (10–15 years ago) were not traditionally accepting of lesbian parenting. Now, the trend is apparently changing, as the lesbian community is beginning to consider the female whole-life experience. She briefly touches on male/female and female/female split-ups and what happens to the child involved. "Flommy" comes from the word *Teflon* "as this non-biological live-in parent thinks it makes her sound less "fabricated."

233. Erlichmann, Karen Lee. "Lesbian Mothers: Ethical Issues in Social Work Practice." *Women & Therapy* 8:1–2 (Fall 1988): 207–24.

As the traditional two-parent family is no longer the normative measure, political and social changes have been made in order to integrate (and make acceptable) new forms of parenting. However, such changes have not yet begun to decrease the stigmatization and discrimination directed toward lesbian mothers. This article argues that social workers must be sensitive to issues that specifically affect lesbian mothers in order to be of service to them. It advocates that social workers be well versed on homophobia, sexuality, culture, lifestyle, and family support groups as they affect the lesbian mother.

234. Ferguson, Ann. "Motherhood and Sexuality: Some Feminist Questions." *Hypatia* 1:2 (Fall 1986): 1–22.

Ferguson writes from the point of view of a leftist, lesbian, feminist academic. She gives a useful review of the other essays in this issue of *Hypatia* (see 53), concisely discusses feminist theory's relation to Freud and looks at feminist ethical questions on motherhood and sexuality. These questions include alternative lifestyles for feminists, issues of bisexuality and celibacy and how one can mother in a patriarchal society. She feels that feminist theorists need to develop a distinctive socio-biology of their own and goes on to refer to numerous other authors and their studies, offering a rich resource for extended research. See 37, 38 for other pieces by Ferguson.

235. Gibson, Gifford Guy. *By Her Own Admission: A Lesbian Mother's Fight to Keep Her Son*. Garden City, N.Y.: Doubleday, 1977.

Based on the first known jury trial (1975) involving the custody rights of a lesbian parent, Gibson recounts, in collaboration with Mary Joe Risher, one mother's horrendous fight and eventual loss of custody of her son. Basically a descriptive case study, the trial transcripts show the sexist, biased view of the courts.

236. Gibbs, Elizabeth D. "Psychosocial Development of Children Raised by Lesbian Mothers: A Review of Research." *Women & Therapy* 8:1–2 (Fall 1988): 65–75.

This article strongly supports lesbian mothers and their ability to be "fit" parents. In light of several recent custody battles that resulted in lesbian mothers losing their children because their lifestyles were viewed by the courts as immoral and detrimental to their offspring, this article attempts to point to reasons why a child's social and psychological development is not stunted by his/her lesbian mother. The strongest reason supported by Gibbs is that lesbian mothers share many of the same concerns that heterosexual mothers have. However, Gibbs is quick to remind us that because their lifestyle is constantly judged negatively by society, lesbian mothers have "special" concerns as well.

237. Goodman, Bernice, ed. *The Lesbian: A Celebration of Difference.* Brooklyn, N.Y.: Out & Out Books, 1977.

Several of the essays in this book compare and contrast lesbian and heterosexual mothers. Particular issues focus on guilt toward one's children and the development of these children. The author suggests that support groups within the lesbian community be formed to assist these mothers.

238. Hanscombe, Gillian E., and Jackie Forster. *Rocking The Cradle: Lesbian Mothers: A Challenge in Family Living.* Boston: Alyson Publications, 1982.

This book deals with the problems confronting lesbians who wish to either become mothers or retain their children in the face of divorce and custody battles. Hanscombe looks at the special problems confronting these otherwise ordinary mothers, such as extreme bias in the family court system. The 1987 edition contains a new introduction. See Beck (230) for a review of this work.

239. Hitchens, Donna J., and Ann Thomas, eds. *Lesbian Mothers and Their Children: An Annotated Bibliography of Legal and Psychological Materials.* San Francisco, Calif.: Lesbian Rights Project, 1980.

This practical annotated bibliography was compiled in 1980 as a sourcebook for lesbian mothers and their advocates. It is a tool with a specific purpose--providing legal support to lesbian mothers--and so is edited with a sense of directness and urgency. Readable and concise, it outlines court cases, journal articles and other sources that provide evidence and precedents for "good enough" lesbian mothering. Although somewhat dated, this book may still be a crucial and powerful source for many women, lawyers and healthcare workers.

Joseph, Gloria. "Mothers and Daughters: Traditional and New Perspectives." *Sage* 1:2 (Fall 1984): 17–21. See 116 for annotated entry.

Klein, Carole. *Mothers and Sons*. Boston: Houghton Mifflin, 1984. See 137 for annotated entry.

240. Lyons, Terrie A. "Lesbian Mothers' Custody Fears." *Women & Therapy* 2 (Summer-Fall 1983): 231–240.

Focusing on the stereotypes and misconceptions the general public has about lesbians, this article tries to convince the reader to think of lesbians as ordinary people. With this in mind, the author draws similarities between lesbian and heterosexual mothers, stressing that both groups of women share the problems of childcare, housing, employment and other economic woes. Furthermore, the author argues that custody battles involving lesbians have only recently come to the surface as a result of the women's and gay movements.

241. Mosely, Leigh. "Lesbian Co-parents and Their Daughters Share Experiences." *Off Our Backs* 14 (July 1984): 2–3+.

This article recaps and provides interesting excerpts from a conference sponsored by the Baltimore Lesbian Mother's Support Group and the Daughters of Lesbians. In this article, lesbian mothers, non-biological lesbian mothers and their children addressed topics of developing rights (within the political system), medical technology of insemination, co-parenting issues, children and teenagers. The discussion generated by the teen panel turned out to be the most revealing and painful. Society pressures and perceptions were discussed as well.

242. Mucklow, Bonnie M., and Gladys K. Phelan. "Lesbian and Traditional Mothers' Responses to Adult Response to Child

Behavior and Self-Concept." *Psychological Reports* 44:3 (1979): 880–882.

A study of 34 lesbian and 47 traditional mothers in the Denver area was conducted to see if significant differences existed between the two groups in terms of maternal attitude and self-concept. The authors found that there were no significant differences either in response to children's behavior or in the self-concept of lesbian and traditional mothers. They conclude that these mothers are probably more similar than different. This study was also analyzed by Judith Miller, et al. in the *Journal of Homosexuality* 7:1 (1981): 49–56.

243. Pollack, Sandra, and Jeanne Vaughn, eds. *Politics of the Heart: A Lesbian Parenting Anthology*. Ithaca, N.Y.: Firebrand Books, 1987.

The two editors point out that there have always been lesbian mothers of various kinds but that until recently many came from heterosexual relationships and often feared losing their children. Now, many single lesbians and lesbian couples are choosing to raise their own children. Moving away from issues of custody, one can now study the effects of lesbian parenting: does it offer a radical alternative to traditional upbringing; how does one deal with homophobia; what are the roles of co-mothers? The book is divided into eight sections including ones on survival, which deals with outside pressures such as the courts; choices, which looks at the social and political implications of motherhood; co-parenting, which focuses on the concerns of the other mother with an interesting look at how lesbian mothers have turned *to* the courts to sort out their own custody battles; conflict, which addresses the fragmentation of many lesbian mothers' lives and "working it out,"which shows how lesbian mothers explore a variety of issues with their children. This is an interesting anthology with a good bibliography on lesbian parenting, including an essay by Beck, 230.

244. Rafkin, Louise, ed. *Different Daughters: A Book by Mothers of Lesbians*. San Francisco: Cleis Press, 1987.

Louise Rafkin has edited a collection of interviews, poems and prose by 25 mothers of lesbian daughters. The constant refrain, which can be heard throughout these pieces, is one of love and acceptance, regardless of the difficulties some families experienced in dealing with their daughter's choice of lifestyle.

245. Rights of Women Custody Group. *Lesbian Mothers on Trial: A Report on Lesbian Mothers & Child Custody.* London: Rights of Women, 1984.

This report looks at the prejudice and discrimination against lesbian mothers. A survey of 36 lesbian mothers, it is concerned with child custody and access disputes. It also offers a comparative study of lesbian mothers in the United States and Australia. The work includes further readings and contacts relating to lesbian issues as well as the questionnaire used in the survey and a summary of recommendations, both legal and general, regarding mothering by lesbians. Some of these recommendations are that a mother's sexual identity not be a factor in custody decisions nor that lesbianism be assumed as harmful to children. Various studies are cited in which it is shown that children are not harmed by living with their lesbian mothers. Previous legal discussions and historical backgrounds to custody disputes are also included.

246. Rohrbaugh, Joanna Bunker. "Choosing Children: Psychological Issues in Lesbian Parenting." *Women & Therapy* 8:1–2 (Fall 1988): 51–64.

Lesbians entering parenthood share many of the same concerns as heterosexual mothers entering parenthood. Issues of timing, day care, career planning, the nuclear family and the extended family are confronted by *all* mothers; however, the lesbian mother must also deal with concerns that are specific to her chosen lifestyle (see Beck, 230). The first-time lesbian parent must come to terms with her lesbian identity, relationships with her parents and other members of the family and bonds with mates or possible co-parents. The author suggests that prospective lesbian mothers analyze their feelings with respect to these areas of concern in order to prepare themselves for this new role.

247. Schaffer, Teya. "Mothering in the Lesbian Community." *Off Our Backs* 14 (July 1984): 4–5.

This brief article offers a number of ideas on women, children and mothering in the lesbian community in efforts to stimulate debate in these areas. It is written by a lesbian mother of a male child. Although a personal account, many broad issues are raised, especially in relation to children. Schaffer discusses her conflicts with raising a "male child" and societal beliefs that boys need male figures to look up to.

248. Schulenburg, Joy A. *Gay Parenting*. Garden City, N.Y.: Anchor Press/Doubleday, 1985.

As a lesbian mother raising her daughter with two gay co-parents, the author could find no general resource to help her cope with the issues of having and raising children. Although many books addressed gay parents with children by previous marriages or addressed individual issues of parenting, none spoke to both gay men and lesbians, on the issue of childbearing from a long-term, non-gender-based perspective. To fill that gap, Schulenburg, who came out at age fourteen, generated a database of questionnaires, letters and conversations from all over the country that became the basis of this book. A mix of statistical, anecdotal and personal insights, her work examines the double bind of being a gay parent, the impact of gay parenting on lovers, children and family and the array of options involved with artificial insemination, co-parenting, marriage, adoption and foster parenting. She also addresses AIDS and legal problems and includes an excellent list of resources.

249. Steinhorn, Audrey. "Lesbian Mothers—the Invisible Minority: Role of the Mental Health Worker." *Women and Therapy* 1:4 (1982): 35–48.

Steinhorn gives a broad picture of the lesbian mother and the particular issues relating to her lesbianism, her mothering and the development of her children. She looks at the pros and cons of remaining "closeted," especially in relation to children. A few custody cases are also reviewed.

250. Valeska, Lucia. "If All Else Fails, I'm Still A Mother" (1985) in Joyce Trebilcot, ed. *Mothering: Essays in Feminist Theory.* Totowa, N.J.: Rowman & Allanheld, 1984, pp. 70–78.

Valeska is a lesbian mother who voluntarily gave up custody of her three children and who looks at mothering from a "childfree" viewpoint. She believes that to have our own biological children is irresponsible and that we should take care of existing children. This article was first published in *Quest* 1:3 (Winter 1975). See Glubka (157) for another mother who gave up custody of her children.

251. Wyland, Francie. *Motherhood, Lesbianism and Child Custody.* Toronto: Wages Due Lesbians, 1977.

This brief but powerful booklet argues that housewives (as well as other unpaid or underpaid mothers) and lesbian mothers should be allies, because all are victims of the lie that the natural way for women to live is as unwaged workers in a heterosexual family unit. This double-edged sword cuts poor mothers by trapping them in marriages based on financial survival, and it cuts lesbian mothers by defining them as unnatural and therefore unfit mothers. This basically Marxist polemic makes a special appeal to lesbians to avoid separatism, which, Wyland argues, merely pits poor heterosexual mothers against their lesbian counterparts. A good list of resources, including sister "Wages Due" organizations, appears at the end.

BIBLIOGRAPHY— BLACK MOTHERS, DAUGHTERS AND SONS

252. Austin, Roy. "Race, Father Absence and Female Delinquency." *Criminology* 15:4 (1978): 487–504.

Austin offers a contrary opinion to the Moynihan Report (1965) that black families without fathers fail. He also refutes the findings of Datesman and Scarpitti (255) that, with the exception of family related offenses, there is no relation between female delinquency and broken homes. Austin's research has shown that a strong mother-daughter bond has an effect on the behavior of the daughter and is related to curtailing delinquency for both black and white girls. He says that the lack of a father in a poor socio-economic environment, i.e., the black family, is conducive to strong mother daughter-bonds whereas in the white middle-class family this father absence poses a problem: there is a stigma attached to father absence, in middle and upper middle-class white families which does not exist for the black family. According to Austin, black daughters of absent fathers actually incur a "special protection" against delinquency due to a close mother-daughter bond. Austin concludes, in contrast to Datesman and Scarpitti, that there is a relationship between father absence and involvement in personal offenses including theft, vandalism and assault and that this relationship is stronger for white girls than for either black girls or boys of either race. It is interesting to note that Datesman and Scarpitti (see below) also found "morals" offenses higher for white girls from father-absent families.

253. Beckett, Joyce O. "Working Wives: A Racial Comparison." *Social Work* (November 1976): 463–471.

Although primarily written for social workers, this is a fascinating essay which uncovers many differences in the working patterns of white and black wives. It summarizes the research conclusions from nine survey studies and census data collected after 1960 in order to investigate the attitudes of black and white husband-wife families toward wives working outside the home. Beckett points out that because white women constitute the overwhelming majority of the total women in any category, the changes for all women reflect white women's' working patterns. However, it was found that black wives have higher rates of labor force participation than do white wives and that among black wives who work full-time these women tend to be from more stable and better-educated families. Their husbands are more likely to be employed and have a higher income than the husbands of black wives who do not work outside the home. The opposite is true for white families: white wives who work fulltime tend to have greater marital instability and husbands with lower educational levels and lower annual earnings. It was also found that black women seem to have more confidence than do white in their ability to pursue an occupation after marriage and that black husbands are more than twice as likely as white to prefer that their wives work. As noted by Rudd and McKenry (221) the wives' perceptions of their husbands' attitudes significantly influenced their working patterns. However, black wives were less influenced than the white wives by their husbands' negative attitudes. Another interesting point which Beckett makes is that black families are more traditional in their ideas about family interaction but more egalitarian in their actual behavior while white families are more egalitarian in ideology and more traditional in behavior.

Birns, Beverly, and Dale Hay, eds. *The Different Faces of Motherhood*. New York: Plenum Press, 1988. See 10 for annotated entry.

254. Brewer, Rose M. "Black Women in Poverty: Some Comments on Female-Headed Families." *Signs* 13:21 (1988): 331–339.

Brewer's stated purpose in this well-documented essay is to place the current debate on poor black women heading households within a structural and political economic context. She notes that blacks have one of the highest rates of unemployment in the country and the relationship between cultural/familial and political/economic spheres is central to understanding the persistence of poverty in the majority of black female-headed households. Brewer notes that there is virtually little difference in the educational attainment of workers today yet there are still great differences in the median income between the sexes and races. Brewer concludes that black female-headed households have become the logical end-product of a series of social, political and economic forces. Wherein the white nuclear family has been sustained and protected historically by the state, the black family has been consistently disrupted by external forces. An interesting point that Brewer makes is that one of the most distinct differences between blacks and other groups is related to household forms. The inclusive black family system of extended relations, out-of-marriage births and female-headed households has been necessary in a context where external disruptions are more powerful than the internal grouping.

Chapman, Jane Roberts, and Margaret Gates, eds. *Women into Wives. The Legal and Economic Impact of Marriage.* Beverly Hills and London: Sage Publications, 1977. See 264 for annotated entry.

255. Datesman, Susan, and Frank Scarpitti. "Female Delinquency and Broken Homes." *Criminology* 13:1 (1975): 505–528.

Datesman and Scarpitti state that the structure of black families mitigates the effect of broken homes on female children. Matrifocal families socialize the daughters to be strong because males are not to be counted on for support. When the types of criminal offenses are controlled and studied, which is often not the case, these authors found that only "morals" offenses are higher for girls from broken homes than for the general population. These types of offenses include running away and bad behavior within the family. They are more common for white female adolescents. Although structure of the home is more important in the female's development than the male's, Datesman and Scarpitti found no particular relationship between broken homes and female delinquency except for family related offenses. See Austin (252) who credits this study for its breakdown of the relationship between broken homes and delinquency by race, sex and type of offense while disagreeing with many of its conclusions.

Fox, Greer Litton, and Judith K. Inazu. "The Influence of Mother's Marital History on the Mother-Daughter Relationship in Black and White Households." *Journal of Marriage and Family* 44 (February 1982): 143–154. See 109 for annotated entry.

256. Harrison, Algea Othella, and JoAnne Holbert Minor. "Interrole Conflict, Coping Strategies, and Role Satisfaction Among Single and Married Employed Mothers." *Psychology of Women Quarterly* 6:3 (Spring 1982): 354–360.

In this study single and married black mothers were compared by the type of coping strategy which they used to handle mother and worker role conflicts as well as the level of satisfaction with each of these roles. It was found that single mothers were significantly more satisfied with their roles as workers than were married working mothers. In terms of coping strategies, married mothers tended to change their internal expectations when faced with a conflict between mothering and worker roles while single mothers attempted to improve the quality of their role performances.

257. Joseph, Gloria I. "Black Mothers and Daughters: Their Roles and Functions in American Society" in Gloria I. Joseph and Jill Lewis, eds. *Common Differences: Conflicts in Black & White Feminist Perspectives*. New York: Anchor Press/Doubleday, 1981, pp. 75–126.

Joseph offers an analysis of black mothers and daughters which takes into consideration the differences of black and white culture. These differences include racial and economic oppression and the fact that the extended family in black culture often takes on the role of the mother. Data from a nationwide survey of black women that Joseph herself conducted are used. She found that 95% of the women interviewed respected their mothers in terms of strength and ability to survive. These same daughters have been socialized to become strong, independent women due to their often precarious circumstances (see Austin 252 and Datesman and Scarpitti 255 for similar findings). Joseph states that there is little available research on black women, including black mothers and daughters, outside of literature. She gives a short history of women in Africa and looks at the contradictions in black culture, as in white, in regard to the idealization and degradation of the mother.

Joseph, Gloria. "Mothers and Daughters: Traditional and New Perspectives." *Sage* 1:2 (Fall 1984): 17–21. See 116 for annotated entry.

258. Lerner, Gerda. *Black Women in White America: A Documentary History*. New York: Random House, 1972.

This book includes oral histories from as early as 1844 to the present. Many of the sections, which include "Slavery," "Survival is a Form of Resistance" and "Black Women Speak of Womanhood" include pieces on mothering from the perspective of the black woman. It cannot be ignored that at least until recent history the black mother has experienced a different set of circumstances than her white counterpart.

259. Lewis, Diane K. "The Black Family: Socialization and Sex Roles." *Phylon* 36 (1975): 221–237.

This article looks at sex-role socialization in black families to see whether there is a distinctive Afro-American culture which can be seen in child-rearing practices. Current studies are inconclusive, although many affirm that mothers have higher expectations of their daughters, demanding more responsibility than from their sons.

Safilios-Rothschild, Constantina. "The Parents' Need for Child Care" in Pamela Roby, ed. *Child Care—Who Cares: Foreign and*

Domestic Infant and Early Childhood Development Policies. New York: Basic Books, 1973. See 279 for annotated entry.

260. Stack, Carol. *All Our Kin: Strategies for Survival in a Black Community.* New York: Harper & Row, 1974.

This is a study of black family life in an urban community in the Midwest which was done by a young white researcher who used "assistants" within the community for observation as well as her own observation and record taking. Stack analyzed the interpretations which the blacks in her study had of their own cultural patterns. Her findings included evidence of strong, positive matrifocal relations as part of extensive kinship relations within the black community whereby the mothers and daughters as well as aunts, sisters and grandmothers are responsible for family life, which consists primarily of women and children.

Walker, Henry A. "Black-White Differences and Family Patterns" in Sanford M. Dornbusch and Myra H. Strobers, eds. *Feminism, Children, and the New Families.* New York: Guilford, 1988, pp. 87–112. See 267 for complete book annotation.

VII.

Mothering and the Family: A Time of Change

The American nuclear family is an integral aspect of patriarchy. The politics involved in the family concern relations of power between husbands and wives, parents and children, as well as between the family and the governing system. According to Letty Pogrebin (277), one of the keys to family politics is the promotion of motherhood, but only for certain types of women. She notes that although Medicare abortions are being denied to poorer women, many of these same women are pressured with sterilization while white middle-class women, who are fighting to retain the rights to abortion for all women, are pressured to reproduce and stay at home with their children.

There are conservative views on the mother's role in the family, even among feminists. Mary Jo Bane (262) and Jean Bethke Elshtain (269) both believe that mothers are the best people to take care of their children. Even if improvements are made in social services and assistance payments, this viewpoint still puts tremendous psychological pressure on women. Other writers such as Jessie Bernard (263), Laura Lein (275), Constantina Safilios-Rothschild (279) and Arlene and Jerome Skolnick (280) offer more liberating ideas. They look at the effects of exclusive childrearing by mothers on the mothers themselves as well as on their children. They all conclude that working, or at least participating in some activity other than mothering, benefits both mothers and children.

The Skolnicks note that the romanticization of motherhood continues to keep women at home, either by choice or through the pressures of societal values. It is this same kind of thinking, although along the more fundamental lines of biology, which informs the writings of Alice Rossi. Rossi's article (278) and certain critiques of it (see 265, 266) constitute an important part of current feminist thinking about the family. Rossi's biological determinism, whereby she believes a woman's role in the family is determined by her ability to reproduce, has been highly criticized. Although most of these writers have praised Rossi for her intellectual contributions, they are afraid that her ideas will be used by anti-feminist, pro-family advocates. Women may be the only ones who can reproduce children, but they are not the only means by which these children can be mothered. Until this romantic myth is dispelled, adequate day care and shared parenting will not become realities.

The Journal of Marriage and the Family, *The Journal of Family Issues* and various other psychological and sociological journals report on family matters and many offer articles referring to mothers and children. A few are in this chapter, as well as in other sections of this bibliography, particularly that on single mothers. Sanford Dornbusch and Myra Strober's recent collection of essays, *Feminism, Children, and the New Families* (267), offers a comprehensive look at contemporary issues concerning women and their families as does an earlier book edited by Rose Laub Coser, *The Family: Its Structures and Functions* (New York: St. Martin's, 1974). The *Current Population Reports* available from the U.S. Government Printing Office are also useful in studying family trends.

At present there is no consensus of what constitutes a family: is one person a family, are dual-career childless couples, how do extended caregivers fit in and what about unmarried partners? While the "moral majority" and pro-life movements applaud the traditional nuclear family, one of their strongest proponents refuses to support the needs of all families.[1]

Note

1. Holmes, Steven. "Bush Will Veto Bill Requiring Job Leave for Care of Family." *New York Times*, May 8, 1990.

BIBLIOGRAPHY—FAMILY

261. Aldous, Joan, ed. *Two Pay Checks: Life in Dual-Earner Families*. Beverly Hills: Sage, 1982.

This book grew from a special issue of *Family Issues* (June 1981). In her opening chapter, "From Dual-Earner to Dual-Career Families" (11–26), Aldous notes that there is an unequal division of labor at home between two-earner couples as well as a paradox between "dual-career" and "family" as the two are not compatible due to the lack of adjustment in most workplaces. There is also a difference between dual-career and dual-earning but the biggest change in recent decades is in the decrease of traditional families. All of the 12 chapters are a good source for further reading on these specific subjects and include reviews of current research. Janet and Larry Hunt in their chapter "Dual-Career Families: Vanguard of the Future or Residue of the Past" (14–58) found three types of couples: traditionalists who do not question traditional sex-role destinies even in dual-earner families; prioritizers who reject current gender arrangements and integrators who consist of couples who work together and, consequently, function on their own without the usual workplace and family dilemmas. In a piece by Joseph Pleck (see 215 for another entry by Pleck), "Work Schedules and Work-Family Conflict" (63–87), it is noted that husbands with working wives have less stressful work schedules and work a shorter week than husbands of homemakers. In "Women's Jobs and Family Adjustment" (129–144), the authors Chanya Piotrkowski and Paul Crits-Christoph found that job satisfaction positively correlates to family adjustment for working wives (see Rudd and McKenry 221 for similar findings). Suzanne Model in her article, "Housework by Husbands: Determinants and Implications" (193–205), found that only when wives' earnings approach those of their husbands does participation in household tasks equalize.

262. Bane, Mary Jo. *Here To Stay: American Families In The Twentieth Century*. New York: Basic Books, 1976.

Bane believes that family ties and commitments will and should continue to persist in western civilization and that public policy should be geared to this fact. Her more innovative ideas include insurance for single parents so that, upon divorce, the woman is automatically covered and, consequently does not suffer from a lowering of income and status. Bane does not believe that parental care can ever be replicated by day care and is basically conservative in her views. She sees the resolution to the conflict between family privacy and social values as lying in the rights of individuals whereby parents are primarily responsible for their children. The book includes an extensive bibliography on the family which is both contemporary and historical.

263. Bernard, Jessie Shirley. *The Future of Marriage*. New Haven: Yale University Press, 1972.

Bernard looks at the fact that each marriage is really made up of two marriages: the husband's and the wife's. She finds that more wives than husbands are discontent with their marriages and that women perceive more problems than do men. The author includes extensive sections of references and notes that are keyed to each chapter as well as tables such as "The happiness of husbands' marriages." Although much of the research is pre-1970, this book is still an important early feminist contribution to work on the family.

264. Chapman, Jane Roberts, and Margaret Gates, eds. *Women into Wives. The Legal and Economic Impact of Marriage*. Beverly Hills and London: Sage Publications, 1977.

This is a collection with an introduction by Jessie Bernard (see 8, 9, 263, 298) of eleven essays concerned with the impact of the institutions of marriage and the family on women. Most of the authors offer suggestions for change either in family structures, social policies or legal issues. "Black Women and the Family" by Diane Holland Painter looks at the effects of racism and poverty on the majority of black women born in America. These are additional (to that of being female) discriminations that black women encounter which negatively affect their family and work lives. "Public Policy in the Family: A New Strategy for Women as Wives and Mothers" by Shelia Kamerman (see 59, 197, 204, 289) points out that there is no single consistent public policy regarding the family in the United States and suggests establishing a family policy which addresses the inequalities and inadequacies faced by women. "Woman into Mothers" by Madeleine Kornfein et al. is annotated separately, see 57.

265. Cerullo, Margaret, Judith Stacey and Winnie Breiens. "Alice Rossi's Sociobiology and Anti-Feminist Backlash." *Berkeley Journal of Sociology* 22 (1977–1978): 167–177.

The authors fault Rossi for her biological determinism and feel that she undermines the transfer of the family and sex roles from the realm of biology to that of society and history. They feel that anti-feminists will use Rossi's theories as validation of the nuclear family, which feminists criticize for its role in participating in women's inequality. This is a very critical piece which needs close reading in relation to Rossi's article, "A Biosocial Perspective of Parenting" (278).

266. Chodorow, Nancy. "Consideration on a Biosocial Perspective on Parenting" (278). *Berkeley Journal of Sociology* 22 (1977–1978): 179–197.

Chodorow states that much of this article is excerpted from her book, *The Reproduction of Mothering* (19). She points out that although Rossi's goals of returning parenting to the center of social organization and protecting women from harmful work and medical conditions are good, Rossi ignores the fact that women's mothering is central to the reproduction of male dominance. Chodorow concludes that women's position is not biologically determined, it can be changed by a re-organization of parenting.

267. Dornbusch, Sanford M., and Myra H. Strober, eds. *Feminism, Children, and the New Families.* New York: Guilford, 1988.

This book contains a large and diverse amount of thought-provoking feminist writing on the American family which the two editors concisely review and summarize in the opening chapter, "Our Perspective." It is possibly the most important book to be published on this topic in recent years. Part I addresses the relationship between feminist ideology and the functioning of families as they affect individual family members. Part II focuses on the "new families," referring to "traditional" families as now being the minority in America, and the increase of variant family forms which has affected mothers, fathers, children and social policies. The final chapter by Dornbusch and Strober, "Public Policy Alternatives," examines the various policy suggestions offered in the preceding chapters with the consensus that most are helpful to children, mothers and fathers. A wide range of topics are covered, such as the effects of maternal employment and divorce on children, including an essay by Lenore Weitzman (see 176), single-parent and stepfamilies, two-earner families, childcare issues, a comparison of black and white family patterns, etc. Each of the 14 chapters contains a summary and short list of references. Many of the essays include critical reviews of current literature, in particular that of Jean Bethke Elshtain (269), and other pieces which are annotated herein. "The War over the Family" by Susan Cohen and Mary Katzenstein concludes that although the family has been the battleground between feminists and the right, the issue is really the roles of men and women in society, not whether the family should be abolished. See 153, 212, 225 for individually annotated essays from this volume.

268. Ehrenreich, Barbara. "On Feminism, Family and Community." *Dissent* 30: 1 (1983): 103–109.

This article includes Ehrenreich's review of Jean Bethke Elshtain's "rambling, pretentious essay" which was published in *Dissent* 29: 4 (1982) (269), as well as a response from Elshtain. Ehrenreich summarizes Elshtain's ideas as being similar to "backyard" populism and late 19th century conservative feminism whereby homebound women planned to change the world by their superior morals. In order to achieve the "social feminism" which Elshtain advocates, Ehrenreich points out that most publicly sponsored social services, such as day care, would have to be eliminated. Ehrenreich goes on to discredit many of Elshtain's statements, particularly those which relate to feminism being anti-family, by showing their lack of context and credibility. She does not disagree with Elshtain's desire for a feminist movement encompassing values associated with women's traditional roles of nurturance and caring but rather, the fact that Elshtain feels these values can only be created by women staying at home in the traditional family. In her response, Elshtain insists that she speaks as a feminist from the political left and accuses Ehrenreich of trying to "squash debate among feminists and radicals on contested and vital matters." Elshtain goes on to defend herself against Ehrenreich's criticisms without actually explaining her pro-family, mother-at-home stance. Another critique of Elshtain's essay by Marshall Berman appears in the spring issue of *Dissent* 30: 2 (1983): 247–255, in which the author discusses Elshtain's views in a broader context of feminist ideology.

269. Elshtain, Jean Bethke. "Feminism, Family and Community." *Dissent* 29: 4 (1982): 442–449.

The author writes as a feminist who is discontent with the way the family has been treated in the majority of feminist writing since the 1960s. Elshtain feels that rather than transforming the human community, women have been encouraged to follow the paths of men. She proposes a course of social feminism, which takes in the needs of all people, including children. There is an implicit assumption in Elshtain's writing that if families were adequately provided for, women would prefer to stay home with their children and only women, not men, would be interested in doing this. See Ehrenreich's response to this article in *Dissent* 30: 1 (268) and Dornbusch and Strober's references (267).

270. Gittins, Diana. *The Family in Question: Changing Households and Familiar Ideologies*. London: Macmillan, 1985.

The Family in Question focuses on family issues such as how families have changed in recent years, patriarchal relations within family life and the gap between ideology, stemming from 19th-century urban bourgeois, and the reality of the family today, which Gittins perceives as creating a "crisis" within contemporary families. Gittins points out that ideologies concerning the family change as well as the actual patterns of family life and she investigates the relationship between these two, particularly how one influences the other. For example, patriarchal relations ensure that the "egalitarian" family cannot exist. The book aims to deconstruct popular myths surrounding the family while offering current studies on family life from a variety of viewpoints including feminist, sociological and historical.

271. Grizzle, Anne F. *Mother Love, Mother Hate: Breaking Dependent Love Patterns in Family Relationships*. New York: Fawcett Columbine, 1988.

Grizzle looks at the problems of "devoted families" and over-involved parenting, which result in a lack of independence for individual family members and children. A large amount of fighting is the usual outcome for these types of families. Grizzle found that as more independent action is achieved, there will often be less fighting but more disagreements. The key in making this transition is persistent caring and commitment. Grizzle, a psychotherapist specializing in family therapy, has written this as a resource and self-help book for people in close-knit families who are experiencing or trying to prevent problems stemming from "dependent love patterns." She sees the first intimate relationship of the mother and child as containing the most intense love-hate feelings which continue throughout our lives.

272. Gross, Harriet Engle, et al. Introduction to "Considering a Biosocial Perspective on Parenting" (278). *Signs* 4: 4 (Summer 1979): 695–717.

This is a critique of Rossi's article by Jessica Bernard, Alice Dan, Nona Glazer, Judith Lorber, Martha McClintock and Niles

Newton with an introduction by Harriet Gross and a reply from Rossi, all of which stem from a special session of the Sociologists for Women in Society on Rossi's article. Gross acknowledges the intellectual significance of Rossi's work while questioning her logic. Bernard does not believe the maternal role is an adequate core for a modern female world but does feel Rossi's work is important in understanding the structure of such a world. Dan agrees with Rossi that biological differences do not have to be used against women and that we cannot ignore these differences, but feels that Rossi takes too much for granted. The consensus of this article is a tribute to Rossi's intellect coupled with a constructive feminist critique of her theories.

273. Howe, Louise, ed. *The Future of the Family: Mothers, Fathers, and Children*. New York: Simon & Schuster, 1972.

This book is a compilation of articles, primarily written in 1971, about American families. Much of it relates to issues pertaining to mothering and includes prose pieces, interviews with working-class and economically deprived women, meetings of divorced and single mothers, journal entries and a popular press piece, "Motherhood: Who needs it?" by Betty Roland (*Look*, March 16, 1971), which surprisingly debunks the notion of the "motherhood myth." Also included is "Women and Children: Male Chauvinist Spock Recants—Almost" by Benjamin Spock wherein Spock states that his assumption that only women, i.e., mothers, could take care of their children was in error. In her introduction Howe looks at how women are affected differently by family roles depending upon their economic and marital situation. She believes that the assumption of the male-bread winner society and all the sexist attitudes which derive from that assumption, determine the lives of all families. This family model, Howe says, is the root of all our current problems in society. The consensus of the contributors is that the economy must be changed to meet the needs of American families by providing for children and restructuring work schedules.

274. Laws, Judith Long. "A Feminist Review of The Marital Adjustment Literature." *Journal of Marriage and the Family* 33 (1971): 483–516.

This is a good early article on the roles of women in marriage and motherhood which concludes that marriage is not good for woman due to their dependency on men. It includes an extensive pre-1970 bibliography on the subject.

275. Lein, Laura. *Families Without Villains: American Families in an Era of Change*. Lexington, Mass.: Lexington Books, 1984.

Lein examines 23 dual-earner families with young children as typical of a major change in American society. She looks for their strengths, including shared responsibilities and equal parenting, and investigates how present day institutions could better serve these families. Although Lein focuses on married families with traditional nuclear set-ups, she takes a positive attitude toward working mothers as benefiting their children, their families, themselves and society as a whole.

276. Luxton, Meg. *More Than a Labour of Love: Three Generations of Women's Work in the Home*. Toronto: The Women's Press, 1980.

An interesting study of three generations—1930s, 1950s and 1970s—of working-class families in a small industrial town, Flin Flon, in northern Canada. In this company town the men work in the factory (which does not hire women) and the women are full-time homemakers since there is little other choice. One chapter is on the women's roles as mothers but Luxton's primary concern is with domestic labor and how it has changed during the development of industrial capitalism. Includes a good bibliography.

277. Pogrebin, Letty. *Family Politics. Love and Power on an Intimate Frontier*. New York: McGraw-Hill, 1983.

This book offers an examination of the politics that operate within conventional families, such as the power relations which exist among men, women and children. The answer to the question "Who is in charge of motherhood" exposes the power relations in family politics. The key to these politics is the promotion of motherhood for the correct kind of woman. Good enough mothers are usually those who are white, middle-class and married. There is a double standard of motherhood which says that while girls are not too young to be raped, they are too young to keep their children and while poor black women are threatened with sterilization, white middle-class mothers are pressured to keep reproducing. Pogrebin notes that terms such as "unwed mothers" and "illegitimate children" refer to women and children who are unclaimed by men.

278. Rossi, Alice S. "A Biosocial Perspective on Parenting." *Daedalus* 106: 2 (Spring 1977): 1–31.

In this highly controversial article Rossi suggests that feminists have gone too far in their rejection of the nurturing role. She sees it as a central biological fact that the core function of the family system is to continue humanity through reproduction and childrearing and that we must look at these biosocial factors before pressing toward equality in marriage. Her point is that proposals for changes in parenting and sex roles may not be consistent with the biology of our species. She concludes that the influence of physiological factors on women as a consequence of pregnancy and childbirth make it hard for the male to have the same relationship with the child. She admits that children are isolated at home alone but doesn't make the connection that mothers are isolated as well and that her idea for "child growth centers" would be beneficial to both mothers and children. See Cerullo (265), Chodorow (266) and Gross (272) for critiques of Rossi's ideas.

279. Safilios-Rothschild, Constantina. "The Parents' Need for Child Care" in Pamela Roby, ed. *Child Care—Who Cares: Foreign and Domestic Infant and Early Childhood Development Policies.* New York: Basic Books, 1973.

The author argues that the need for a woman to put aside all of her non-family interests and to spend all her time and energy on childcare is bad for the woman, the children and the marriage. It particularly restricts women from developing their own lives and guarantees them second-class status in society. This is one of 26 articles concerned with child care programs as well as particular problems such as "The Black Child and Child-Care Issues" by John Dill.

280. Skolnick, Arlene, and Jerome Skolnick. *Intimacy, Family and Society*. 2nd ed. Boston: Little, Brown, 1978.

This book was written in response to the current perceptions of a "crisis" within the American family (see Gittins, 270, for a similar view), the crisis being that the traditional family and its values are endangered. The authors suggest that the family is a concept, not a biological reality, and that what we are currently seeing is not a breakdown of the institution of the family but a destruction of the myths surrounding it. The Skolnicks point out that day care can only be viewed as a deprivation to children when motherhood is romanticized and mothers thought to have innate capabilities for the caring of children. They emphasize the need for good quality day care of all kinds (drop-in through full days) as a vital necessity for the well-being of both mothers and children. The book is profusely illustrated with photographs of parents and children. A similar work by these authors is *Family in Transition*. 5th ed. (Boston: Little, Brown, 1986).

281. Thorne, Barrie, ed. *Rethinking The Family: Some Feminist Questions*. New York: Longman, 1982.

This is a book of feminist essays, most originally given as public lectures in 1979 at Stanford University, which were written in response to the ongoing controversy over the family. Unfortunately, feminism and the women's movement are often pointed to as being anti-family. Thorne introduces the 11 essays and gives an overview of feminist theory in relation to the contemporary family and women's place within it. See Chodorow and Contratto's "The Fantasy of the Perfect Mother" (21) and Ruddick's "Maternal Thinking" (81) which have been individually annotated.

VIII.

The Children: A New Generation

As there is a great deal of literature on families, so is there on children: children of divorce, children as a factor in marital satisfaction, abused children. What is offered here is a selection of writings on children which primarily pertain to their experience of mothering. Many articles in the *Journal of Divorce* as well as other journals incorporate studies of children from fatherless families and a few have been included. The researcher wishing to find more information specifically related to the child should pursue a number of good research guides and bibliographies on the subject, including those by Mary Gouke and Arlene Rollins, Mary Nofsinger and Kathleen Watkins.[1] Childhood, like mothering, is too heterogeneous a subject to be covered in one publication.

Alice Miller is one of the most outspoken critics of traditional childrearing practices. In *The Drama of the Gifted Child* (291) she offers the idea that children are often damaged by the parent through the parent's (usually the mother's) narcissistic cathexis of the child whereby she experiences the child as a part of herself. As a result, the child develops a false sense of self which continues into adulthood, thereby affecting the next generation. A mother can only react empathetically to her child if she is free of her own childhood. One line by Miller succinctly summarizes her views: ". . . the parents' childhood tragedy is continued in their children" (291, p. 25).

Children of single mothers, especially single mothers by choice, are possibly better off in some instances, as are the mothers. The child of a single mother who chooses to parent on her own has not had to undergo the traumas and conflicts of divorce nor feel the possible rejection by one parent which the child of separated parents sometimes encounters. Other benefits, such as a less hierarchal family structure and enhanced closeness between mothers and children, have been discussed in the section on single mothers by Robert Weiss (174, 175) and others.

Juliet Mitchell (327) believes that the child's socialization and enculturation is the same as being socialized and encultured into a patriarchal world. Therefore, if there is no male figure present, this process might be somewhat different. In the same way, if a female child sees her mother's preference for the father and thereby wants to be the father (i.e., have a penis) in order to win the mother, this developmental stage might be circumvented if there is no father in the family.

However, some of the negative aspects for children of single mothers include the child being turned into the spouse, an inability of the child to share the mother with other adults and discriminatory labeling in the social and school systems. Both Jean Renvoize (169) and Judith Barker[2] report that labels such as "disadvantaged" and "problem child" are often automatically given to children of single parents, thereby creating expectations of failure. Recent reports from the U.S. Census Bureau state that nearly one out of every four children under six is poor. Reasons given include an increase in the number of single teenage mothers and a shortage of affordable day care.[3]

Nancy Chodorow offers new insights into the female child's development which have been referred to in various other sections of this bibliography. Chodorow believes that because girls do not have to switch from their initial closeness with the mother in order to develop their gender identity, their developmental process is smoother than that of boys who must differentiate from the mother and identify with the father (Chodorow 19, p. 97).

Although Miller, Chodorow and Dinnerstein all offer theories relating to the effects of mothering on children, they are more concerned with the adult who was once a child. Many of the studies which have been done on the relationship between mothers and children in terms of how this affects the children, while they are still children, can be found in *Developmental Psychology* (see Bronstein 284 and Hetherington 287). As noted before, there are also many studies on children of single parents and it is interesting to see the large amount that has been done on children of working mothers, some of which have been annotated in that section of this bibliography.

Notes

1. Gouke, Mary and Arlene McClarty Rollins. *One-Parent Children: The Growing Minority. A Research Guide.* New York: Garland, 1990. Nofsinger, Mary M. *Children and Adjustment to Divorce. An Annotated Bibliography.* New York: Garland, 1990. Watkins, Kathleen Pullan. *Parent-Child Attachment. A Guide to Research.* New York: Garland, 1987.

2. Barker, Judith. "Single Mothers, Powerlessness and Empowerment: A Class, Race and Sexual Orientation Comparison." Dissertation presented to the Department of Sociology, University of Oregon, 1989.

3. Barden, J.C. "Poverty Rate Is Up for the Very Young." *New York Times*, April 16, 1990.

BIBLIOGRAPHY—CHILDREN

282. Adams, Paul L., Judith R. Miller and Nancy A. Schrepf. *Fatherless Children.* New York: Wiley, 1984.

Although primarily a textbook for child development specialists and mental health workers, *Fatherless Children* contains a useful review of 1970s and early 1980s literature on the subject of children without fathers. A positive change in attitude toward single mothers and their children can be seen to have developed in the literature over the past two decades. See Betty Caldwell (285) for an earlier treatment of children without fathers.

283. Bem, Sandra L. "Gender Schema Theory and Its Implications for Child Development: Raising Gender-aschematic Children in a Gender-schematic Society." *Signs* 8: 4 (Summer 1983): 598–616.

Bem introduces a new theory of sex typing (i.e., the process by which children acquire sex-appropriate behavior). In this gender-schema theory the child inevitably learns his or her culture's definition of maleness and femaleness and then uses these sex-related associations to assimilate new information, hence the reproduction of sexist society. Parents have the opportunity of reducing their own sex-typed behavior and attitudes as well as censoring cultural messages which in turn will alter the basic data from which the child will construct his/her concepts of maleness and femaleness. Bem notes that it is important for parents to provide an alternative view if they want their child to remain gender-aschematic while functioning in a gender-schematic society and suggests that sex differences be taught in relation to anatomy alone. She also points out that many feminist children's books must be held back from the child at first as they often show what is not, while teaching what should be.

284. Bronstein, Phyllis. "Differences in Mothers' and Fathers' Behaviors Toward Children: A Cross-Cultural Comparison." *Developmental Psychology* 20: 6 (1984): 995–1003.

This article studies a number of Mexican families for differences in maternal and paternal behaviors toward children. It was found, contrary to accepted traditional behavior patterns, that fathers were slightly more affectionate to children than mothers, while mothers spent more time attending to children's immediate needs. A significant difference was found in fathers' attitudes toward reprimanding and instructing boy and girl children: more emphasis and instruction were given to boys, fewer reprimands were given to girls. The results found in this Mexican study were consistent with those found in recent studies of American families. Bronstein includes a good recent bibliography on the subject.

285. Caldwell, Betty, and Henry Ricciuti, eds. *Review of Child Development Research.* Vol. 3. Chicago: University of Chicago Press, 1973.

This volume includes a chapter on children in fatherless families and an extensive review of research on the subject prior to 1973, which is interesting to study for trends in attitudes toward the children of single mothers. See Adams (282) for later research on these children.

Dornbusch, Sanford M., and Myra H. Strober, eds. *Feminism, Children, and the New Families.* New York: Guilford, 1988.

See 267 for complete book annotation. The following chapters particularly pertain to children: Chapter Six, "The Interests of Feminists and Children in Child Care" by Karen Skold (pp. 113–

136), and Chapter 11, "Divorce and Children" by Susan E. Krantz (pp. 249–273).

286. Gilligan, Carol. *Making Connections: The Relational Worlds of Adolescent Girls at Emma Willard School.* Cambridge, Mass.: Harvard University, 1990.

Shortly after Gilligan's ground-breaking work, *In a Different Voice* (324), the Project on the Psychology of Women and the Development of Girls was started by Gilligan and her colleagues at the Harvard Graduate School of Education. Some of the results of this study have been published in this new book which is a collection of essays written both individually and collectively by members of the project. These essays have as their common theme the intention of discovering how adolescent girls relate to themselves and to others and how they experience conflict. The study was conducted through intensive interviews and sentence completion tests. The girls were examined for their attitudes toward friendship, leadership, sexual morality, politics and violence. The findings include the fact that while 11–year-old girls are self-confident with a high sense of integrity, by the time they turn 15 or 16, their response to adolescence reveals a reaction to patriarchal culture which demands their silence. Gilligan and her colleagues have gone on to research ways of developing continuing self-esteem in young girls.

287. Hetherington, E.M. "Effects of Father Absence on Personality Development in Adolescent Daughters." *Developmental Psychology* 7: 2 (1972): 313–326.

This study seeks to examine the effects of father absence on young girls as a result of divorce or death. It found that daughters of divorces sought more attention from males and engaged in heterosexual interaction early. They were also more open and responsive in non-verbal communications toward males. Daughters of widows were found to express the effects of father absence in inhibition, avoidance and restraint around males. The study found, in either case, that early separation from a father figure has worse effects, such as promiscuous behavior, than later separation. Personality scales, childrearing practices, developmental, social and behavioral attitudes were also studied. This article was published in 1973 as "Girls Without Fathers" *(Psychology Today* 6).

288. Jones, Linda M., and Joanne L. McBride. "Sex-Role Stereotyping in Children as a Function of Maternal Employment." *The Journal of Social Psychology* 111 (1980): 219–223.

Forty first and second grade boys and girls, half of whom had working mothers, were questioned on who would be most likely to do a number of adult and children's activities. Although there were no significant sex differences nor differences between first and second graders, the children of non-working mothers gave stereotyped sex-role responses while the responses for the children of working mothers were sex-neutral.

289. Kamerman, Shelia B. "Child Care Services: An Issue for Gender Equality and Women's Solidarity." *Child Welfare* 44: 3 (May-June 1985): 259–271.

This article discusses the issue of childcare as a universal, broad-based problem, with strong ties to women. It is a major economic and political issue that cuts across class, ethnic, radical and ideological lines. The author agrees that the great number of women entering the workforce today have in many ways transformed our society. The need for proper childcare for all classes will lead to greater empowerment of women as a group. Contrary to what one might assume, feminist groups (like NOW) have not put the issue of childcare high on their agendas until recently. Rather, it has been women's organizations such as the National Committee on Jewish Women that have bought childcare to the forefront. In comparison to other countries, the U.S. is far behind in providing adequate care for children; it has been made easily accessible to middle- and upper-class women, as opposed to lower-income mothers who need it most. See Kamerman's other articles, 159, 197, 204, 264.

Lynn, David Brandon. *Daughters and Parents: Past, Present and Future*. Monterey, Calif.: Brooks/Cole, 1979. See 119 for annotated entry.

290. Margolin, Gayla, and Gerald R. Patterson. "Differential Consequences Provided by Mothers and Fathers for Their Sons and Daughters." *Developmental Psychology* 11: 4 (1975): 537–538.

This study investigates how parents respond to their daughters and sons in everyday situations in the home. It found that mothers and fathers were more likely to respond to a like-sex child. It was further observed that fathers reflected increased levels of positive responses to their sons rather than daughters as the child matured. It was implied that there tend to be more father-son than mother-son or mother-daughter likenesses in activities and interests.

291. Miller, Alice. *The Drama of the Gifted Child: The Search For The True Self.* (1979). New York: Basic Books, 1981.

Miller states in her introduction that she is trying to find a way, within the framework of psychoanalysis, for the patient to regain his/her authentic sense of self. Miller, a psychoanalyst for 20 years, believes that many children undergo "narcissistic cathexis" by the mother: they are used to replace the parent's lost childhood and consequently never develop a true sense of themselves. Until one's childhood suffering is acknowledged, Miller says, it will be passed on to the next generation. This is an important book that relates to mothering from a psychoanalytic perspective that is accessible to the average reader. See Miller's other works, 292, 293.

292. Miller, Alice. *For Your Own Good: Hidden Cruelty in Child-Rearing and the Roots of Violence.* (1980). New York: Farrar, Straus & Giroux, 1984.

In her second book Miller looks at modern practices of childrearing and closely studies the childhoods of a teen-age prostitute and heroin addict, Adolf Hitler and Jurgen Bartsch, a child murderer, to see what in their upbringing could lead to such personal and widespread devastation. She finds and chronicles common threads of physical and emotional abuse and humiliation at the hands of one or both parents. She also suggests that Germany's culture of childrearing with its stress on obedience contributed to the "success" of Hitler and Nazism. Miller's thesis is an extension of her ideas in *The Drama of the Gifted Child* (291) wherein the parents are responsible for the actions of their children, to the extent that they have been abused themselves as children. Miller's writings are essential to an understanding of parenting. The book includes a good bibliography on children, particularly battered and abused ones.

293. Miller, Alice. *Thou Shalt Not Be Aware: Society's Betrayal Of The Child.* (1981). New York: Farrar, Straus & Giroux, 1984.

Miller's most recent book, an extension of her previous two (291, 292), looks at psychoanalysis (which Miller practiced for 20 years) and its connection, or dis-connection, to the realities of childhood. Although the chapter "The Pain of Separation and Autonomy" is particularly relevant to mothering, the book is primarily concerned with child abuse. Miller defines child abuse as any humiliation or neglect of the child and points out that the child who has been abandoned by the mother may abandon others as the only way to negate the dependency of childhood. The book includes an extensive bibliography on child abuse literature.

294. Osfsky, Joy D. "Parent-Child Interaction: Daughters' Effects Upon Mothers' and Fathers' Behaviors." *Developmental Psychology* 7: 2 (1972): 157–168.

This study observed a group of 41 five-year-old girls and their parents in a structured setting and found that the girls' behavior had an effect on the parents. The mothers tended to be more encouraging, thus letting the children figure out things on their own. The fathers, on the other hand, were more apt to aid the children, either physically or by helping with an answer to a problem or situation. The author concludes that it is important to continue an investigation of child-parent effects.

295. Stanton, Ann M. *When Mothers Go To Jail.* Lexington, Mass.: Lexington Books, 1980.

Stanton's objective was to study the effects of maternal deprivation on children whose mothers had been sent to jail. She notes that of the estimated 15,000 incarcerated mothers (in 1977), 56% had dependent children living with them prior to their sentencing period. The point is that it is not fair that the children are punished as a consequence of their mothers' actions. Some American institutions even forbid children under 16 or 18 from visiting their mothers, as they believe it is too traumatic for the children. Stanton sees a recent developing interest in establishing residential centers for mothers and children as stemming from a concern for the mothers' reformation, not necessarily the child's welfare, even though statistics show that children of convicts are four times more likely than other children to become criminals themselves. The effects of poverty should of course be taken into consideration here. Stanton points out that incarcerated fathers usually have wives to care for their children while many incarcerated women are single mothers or married to unresponsible husbands; therefore, incarceration is a more severe punishment on women. She recommends preservation of family ties and that criminal punishment should not include destroying family relations. A bibliography on incarcerated mothers and their children is included as well as an appendix of interview questions used for both the children and their mothers. See Baunach (6) for the effects of incarceration on the mothers themselves.

IX.

Feminism: A Framework for Mothering

Although the initial section of this bibliography consists primarily of feminist books on mothering, there are also a number of general works written by feminists which relate to the subject. Most of these books can be divided into three topics: (1) the relation of mothering to patriarchal society, (2) biological theories of mothering and (3) pronatalism.

In the patriarchal system women have very little control over their decision to mother. For example, one woman might be pregnant but doesn't want to have a child, at least at this time. Due to restrictions on abortions, she is forced to give birth. It is true that this woman is not forced to become a mother, but the decision to give up one's child should be a choice no one is forced to make. On the other hand, another woman wants to have a child, but in her case the lack of childcare support prevents her. In a recent national news story one woman's decision to have a child cost her her life. Studies evidently reveal that the victims of abuse are often pregnant wives (Fox Butterfield, *The New York Times*, January 21, 1990).

Azizah Al-hibri (296), Hester Eisenstein (302) and Iris Young (312) all believe that we must understand the fundamental roots of patriarchy in order to change the present system. They point out that shared parenting, better day care and the end to discrimination in the workplace are not enough in themselves to alter the basic structure of male-dominated society. Women cannot take control of decisions regarding their choice to be mothers until the patriarchy is completely disassembled.

Biological determinism can best be defined as women's biological destiny to be mothers. A few feminist theorists, such as Alice Rossi (278) and Jean Bethke Elshtain (269), take the view that this biological feature of women can be used to their advantage; for example, women can enrich their capacity for nurturance through their ability to bear (and hence, raise) children. Many other theorists would disagree. Ruth Bleir (299) and Anne Fausto-Sterling (304) both point out that these bio-sociological ideas have been and will continue to be used to keep women in their place as second-class citizens. They believe that it is not woman's biology that has restricted her but the culture in which she lives. There is too much danger in the theories of biological determinism to think of using them for women's advantage.

Pronatalism is the belief that women should give birth, as they are the only ones who can. And once they give birth, they should also raise the children since motherhood is revered as a superior role within patriarchy, as it is also within matriarchy. Pronatalism is usually thought of as an anti-feminist movement, along the lines of pro-life, yet feminists who promote the idea of matriarchy are basically incorporating pronatalist, or determinist, assumptions into their theories. Martha Gimenez (308) looks closely at feminist writers who, perhaps unwittingly, promote some of these ideas.

Luce Irigaray (115), as do Barbara Love and Elizabeth Shanklin (310), promotes the idea of a matriarchy as the solution to many current societal problems. Women, of course, would benefit greatly from this system but it is hard to fathom how replacing one autocratic system (i.e., patriarchy) with another will improve the whole of society. As early as 1970, Firestone (305) advocated turning women's biological capabilities over to technology as the only way for women to be free. It is an interesting exercise to re-read *The Dialetic of Sex* 20 years later in relation to current technological advances and the controversy over surrogate parenting.

BIBLIOGRAPHY—FEMINISM

296. Al-hibri, Azizah. "Reproduction, Mothering, and the Origins of Patriarchy" (1981) in Joyce Trebilcot, ed. *Mothering: Essays in Feminist Theory*. Totowa, N.J.: Rowman & Allanheld, 1984, pp. 81–93.

The purpose of this essay is to explain the origins, development and present-day manifestations of patriarchal behavior and institutions, of which mothering is one. Regarding mothering, the author offers the premise that the first males resented the woman's childbearing capacities and, as a result, also the child. Consequently, they withdrew from the nurturing process. This article was originally published under the title "Capitalism is an Advanced Stage of Patriarchy; But Marxism is not Feminism" in *Women and Revolution*, edited by Lillian Sargent (Boston: South End Press, 1981).

297. Baruch, Grace, Rosalind Barnett and Karyl Rivers. *Lifeprints: New Patterns of Love and Work for Today's Women*. New York: McGraw-Hill, 1983.

This book is based on a study initiated by the National Science Foundation of how women's well-being is affected by work, marriage, children, homemaking, etc. Over 300 white women between the ages of 35 and 55 responded to a questionnaire which was developed from interviews with 60 women. The authors found that as long as they knew what to expect, women derived satisfaction in a variety of role patterns, i.e., a woman at home with young children should expect to go through periods of feeling undervalued. An important finding was the fact that having children is not a crucial element to a woman's well-being. It is not the number of roles (wife, mother, worker) which is critical but how the woman manages these roles and what are her resources. In a chapter on mothers and daughters it was found that the majority of relationships were warm and caring and that good mother-daughter relationships had a positive effect on the well-being of the adult daughter. The women with the highest degree of well-being were married women with children and prestige jobs. See Hoffman (199) for another study with similar findings and (93, 180 and 314) for other studies by Baruch and Barnett, one of which, 180, is somewhat contradictory to the findings in this work.

298. Bernard, Jessie. *The Female World.* New York: Free Press, 1981.

Part of most female worlds is participation in the role of mother. Bernard's book is written from the point of view that the world around us (i.e., history, science, art and politics) is defined by males. Therefore, we need to certify the world of females. Bernard includes an extensive bibliography (40 pages) on women. Although this is not specifically a book on mothering, Bernard is an important writer whose ideas are central to a feminist theory on mothering. See her other works (8, 9 and 263) in this bibliography.

299. Bleier, Ruth. *Science and Gender: A Critique of Biology and Its Theories on Women.* New York: Pergamon Press, 1984.

Bleier looks at recent socio-biological theories on women's natural role as nurturant mothers, including that of Rossi (278). She finds the research supporting Rossi's theory to have serious political implications as well as "shoddy and deceptive methodology." She says that culture, not biology, has constrained our potential and points out that some feminist and psychoanalytic writing includes socio-biological or determinist assumptions which need to be examined. See Fausto-Sterling (304) for similar arguments.

300. Chodorow, Nancy. "Being and Doing: A Cross-Cultural Examination of the Socialization of Males and Females" (1971) in Vivian Gornick and Barbara Morgan, eds. *Women in Sexist Society: Studies in Power and Powerlessness*. New York: Basic Books, 1971, pp. 173–197.

Chodorow sees two crucial issues relating to the liberation of women and men from current sex roles. First, whether or not there is any truth to the claim that there are biologically determined psychological differences between men and women and, second, why in almost every society women are dominated, usually physically, politically and economically, by men. She refutes the idea of universal differentiation and shows by a comparison of cultures and socialization practices how these differences sometimes do occur. She also attempts to show how the development and socialization of males lead to the devaluation and oppression of women. This essay has also been published in Chodorow's recent book, *Feminism and Psychoanalytic Theory* (318).

301. De Beauvoir, Simone. *The Second Sex*. (1949). New York: Alfred A. Knopf, 1953.

First published in France in 1949 with the most recent printings only containing updated introductions, de Beauvoir's book is still a basic text for beginning any feminist study about women and their place in the patriarchy. She applies an existentialist approach to understanding women's lives and possibilities. De Beauvoir's concept of women as "the other" remains a fundamental part of women's lives today, as does the view that women's primary role is that of mother. Although she sees motherhood as psychologically natural to women, she also sees its limits and proposes accessible childcare as a solution to both the mother's captivity as well as the child's. Her chapter on "The Mother" is largely concerned with women's rights to abortion, still one of the central issues of feminist politics. See two articles on de Beauvoir in *Hypatia* (53) and one by Schwarzer (311), as well as Mitchell's critique (327).

302. Eisenstein, Hester. *Contemporary Feminist Thought*. Boston: G.K. Hall & Company, 1983.

Developed from a course Eisenstein taught at Barnard in the 1970s, this book primarily deals with uncovering the patriarchal power structure and developing a woman-centered analysis. It has been written as a history and critique of feminist thought from 1970 to 1983 with an emphasis on radical feminism. Eisenstein's critiques of Chodorow, Dinnerstein and Rich have been annotated separately in the section on mothering; see 32, 33, 34.

303. Eisenstein, Hester, and Alice Jardine, eds. *The Future of Difference*. Boston: G.K. Hall, 1980.

This is a collection of essays from a conference, "The Scholar and The Feminist VI: The Future of Difference," held at Barnard College in 1979. The editors define differentiation as the psychoanalytic term for the process by which children learn that they are not contiguous with the world. Five essays, one each by Benjamin (315), Chodorow (317), Flax (107), Gallop (320) and Gilligan (323), have been annotated separately.

304. Fausto-Sterling, Anne. *Myths of Gender: Biological Theories About Women and Men*. New York: Basic Books, 1985.

This is a complex book dealing with feminist questions of determinism and bio-sociological arguments that have been used throughout history to keep women in their place. Fausto-Sterling states that the book is both a scientific and political statement. See Bleier (299) for similar arguments and Rossi (278) for an earlier opinion.

305. Firestone, Shulamith. *The Dialetic of Sex: The Case for Feminist Revolution*. New York: Bantam Books, 1970.

Firestone and other radical feminists saw biological motherhood as the heart of women's oppression and felt that women must control technology to be free. Although there are no actual concrete proposals made in this work, Firestone's primary goal is the freedom of women from the tyranny of reproductive biology and the diffusion of childbearing and -rearing to society as a whole. She wants to integrate women and children into society while destroying male/female, adult/child cultural distinctions. See Mitchell's critique of Firestone (327).

306. Friedan, Betty. *The Second Stage*. New York: Summit Books, 1981.

Almost 20 years after the publication of *The Feminine Mystique*, Friedan is confronted with a new generation of daughters who want to know how to incorporate the careers they have been raised to expect with the children they now want. She sees the choices which women have today as lacking a basis in reality; an example is the lack of a national policy on day care and parental leave. Friedan believes that feminists must confront the reality of women's roles in the family. She concludes that we will not bring changes to the workplace and childcare as long as only women are the beneficiaries. See Mitchell's critique of Friedan (327).

307. Gerson, Mary-Joan. "Feminism and the Wish for a Child." *Sex Roles* 11:5/6 (1984): 389–397.

Gerson investigated the motivations for parenthood in 184 unmarried, childless, female college undergraduates and found that positive memories of early childhood maternal love, traditional feminine sex-role identification and anti-feminist beliefs were the primary psychological variables accounting for the wish to have children. Feminism, defined in the study in terms of receptivity to and approval of feminist goals, was found to be negatively related to the motivation for motherhood by a number of researchers besides Gerson. The various measures used in this study are interesting in themselves, such as the "Index of Parenthood Motivation" which consists of six components, including the ranking of childrearing relative to other adult activities and the rating of overall benefits and costs of having children. It was found that although women who subjectively identify with feminism are less interested in becoming mothers, those feminists who did express the desire for a child saw motherhood as offering opportunities for mastery and assertiveness. Rather, the costs of childrearing for feminist women center on a loss of freedom with regard to career aspirations. Gerson also points out that the positive motivation for parenthood of happy childhood memories is inversely related to feminism, i.e., women with feminist sympathies often do not have positive memories of their mothers in early childhood. An earlier version of this article was published as "The Lure of Motherhood" in *Psychology of Women Quarterly* 5:2 (Winter 1980): 207–217. See Gerson's other articles annotated herein, (41, 42 and 43).

308. Gimenez, Martha E. "Feminism, Pronatalism, and Motherhood" (1980) in Joyce Trebilcot, ed. *Mothering: Essays in Feminist Theory*. Totowa, N.J.: Rowman & Allanheld, 1984, pp. 287–314.

Pronatalism can be defined as the support of motherhood, of the bearing and raising of children by women. This article deals with issues of reproduction and calls for feminist acceptance of a childfree status. This point of view is interesting, as other critics of the feminist movement today call for it to have more concern with motherhood. Gimenez offers insightful critiques of other authors who are concerned with pronatalism from a variety of viewpoints including Firestone (305), Mitchell (327), Rossi (278), Judith Blake, Linda Gordon and Lucinda Cisler.

309. Kuykendall, Eleanor H. "Toward an Ethic of Nurturance: Luce Irigaray on Mothering and Power" (1982) in Joyce Trebilcot, ed. *Mothering: Essays in Feminist Theory*. Totowa, N.J.: Rowman & Allanheld, 1984, pp. 263–274.

Kuykendall gives the reader an introduction to "écriture feminine," or feminine writing, from France which sees women's power as deriving from their ability to give birth and promote a feminist ethic of nurturance. Kuykendall believes that Irigaray's proposal for a matriarchy based on nurturance lacks a supporting political analysis. All of the French writers offer complex and interesting views which assume an understanding of both the French psychoanalyst Jacques Lacan as well as Freud.

See Irigaray's "And the One Doesn't Stir without the Other" (115).

310. Love, Barbara, and Elizabeth Shanklin. "The Answer is Matriarchy" (1978) in Joyce Trebilcot, ed. *Mothering: Essays in Feminist Theory*. Totowa, N.J.: Rowman & Allanheld, 1984, pp. 275–283.

Love and Shanklin define matriarchy as a society in which women determine the conditions of motherhood, in which the mode of childrearing is nurturant and in which all relationships are modeled on the mother-child dyad, thereby eliminating patriarchal institutions. In the matriarchal society production serves the interest of reproduction rather than the accumulation of wealth or promotion of war. The authors believe that all contemporary "movements" (women's liberation, children's advocacy, black, lesbian, environmental, etc.) are all movements toward matriarchy. Unfortunately, the authors do not give any concrete suggestions as to how we will easily achieve this blissful state. This essay was first published in *Our Right To Love*, edited by Ginny Vida (Englewood Cliffs, N.J.: Prentice-Hall, 1978.)

311. Schwarzer, Alice. *Simone de Beauvoir Today: Conversations 1972–1982*. London: Chatto & Windus, 1984.

Schwarzer is a West German journalist and feminist who worked with de Beauvoir in France, particularly in the underground abortion movement of the early 1970's. On the question of mothering, de Beauvoir has said that present-day motherhood is not creative but, rather, is a form of servitude. The basis of the male-female division of labor is the concept of feminine maternal nature, which was invented by men. De Beauvoir warns against the mystic status of motherhood and women's nature. She points out that motherhood is not a women's life work and a capacity for biological motherhood does not mean a duty for social motherhood.

312. Young, Iris Marion. "Is Male Gender Identity the Cause of Male Domination?" (1981) in Joyce Trebilcot, ed. *Mothering: Essays*

in Feminist Theory. Totowa, N.J.: Rowman & Allanheld, 1984, pp. 129–146.

Young disputes Chodorow and other contemporary theorists such as Nancy Hartsock and Sandra Harding that male domination is the sole result of women's mothering. She gives a good synopsis of Chodorow's theory of gender development and goes on to look at Harding's and Hartsock's extension of this theory. Young's premise is that gender theory diverts feminist thinking from focusing on the actual structures of male power and domination. She also points out that Chodorow's and Dinnerstein's solution (see 19, 27) of shared parenting is dependent on a total restructuring of male institutions in society, which is not a simple matter.

X.

Psychoanalysis: A Feminist Tool

The premise advanced in *The (M)other Tongue* (322), that an understanding of mothering will extend psychoanalytic theory and lead to a re-interpretation of texts, is key to the importance of many of the works that have been annotated in this bibliography.

Examples of the usefulness of feminist psychoanalytic theory abound. As shown by Shirley Garner et al. (322), it has debunked certain ingrained concepts such as the selfless mother being a necessity for the ideal development of her child. This notion has served patriarchy well by keeping women at home while being detrimental to both women and children. The idea that a woman's well-being is based on her role as a mother is also no longer accepted as valid (Rosalind Barnett and Grace Baruch, 314).

Women's role as nurturer is one of the primary concepts with which feminist psychoanalytic theorists have been concerned. Nancy Chodorow, Carol Gilligan and Jean Baker Miller have all written on the subject. Chodorow (19) says that women develop the ability to empathize which results in their family role becoming centered on taking care of children and men. This role is relational and personal, according to Chodorow, which is the same idea that Gilligan presents in *A Different Voice* (324). Gilligan's thesis is that the female defines herself through her relations to others and judges herself on her ability to care. Although Gilligan's and Miller's works are not directly concerned with mothering, they easily relate to any study on mothers and daughters, women's role as mother, mothers in patriarchy, etc.

Like Gilligan, Jean Baker Miller (326) also sees women's psychological characteristic of nurturing as a strength which has been turned into a weakness. Miller's book is an important early contribution to feminist thought. Miller shows women their subordinate position (as wife and mother) in a male-dominated society because she believes that change can only take place once the current situation has been acknowledged.

Barbara Love and Elizabeth Shanklin (310) point out that the ability to nurture oneself as well as others can only be developed through the experience of having been nurtured. The "motherless" woman may try to deny her loss by the mothering of others but she cannot be a successful parent until her own daughterhood is resolved. These ideas, of course, reflect back on the work of Alice Miller (293) and lead to an analysis of Chodorow's theories on child development.

These theories have opened a new way of seeing. In this theoretical construction, individual development shifts from the oedipal to the pre-oedipal, from the father to the mother. The previous male emphasis was on the separation of the child from the mother. The new feminist emphasis is on the mutual recognition of the mother and child.

The French feminists are concerned with the pre-oedipal relation of the mother and daughter as the basis of their work. These French theorists, who are discussed by Jane Gallop (320) and Juliet Mitchell (327), constitute a branch of psychoanalytic thinking which is quite unique and has not been thoroughly discussed in this section, as many of the books are not available in North America. Another important contribution to feminist psychoanalytic theory has been made by Jessica Benjamin (315, 316). Her thesis that a mother who is not in a subordinate position to either her child or her mate will benefit her child is the basis for much contemporary writing on mothers.

A great deal has been written on object-relations theories which concerns mother-infant relations. Outside of the work of Chodorow, these writings, which deal with psychological issues of dependency and separation, have not been included in this bibliography as they do not directly relate to feminist theories of mothering. The bibliographies compiled by Chodorow (19) and Benjamin (316) contain many references to this subject as do journals such as *Child Development* and *Social Psychology*.

BIBLIOGRAPHY— PSYCHOANALYSIS

313. Alpert, Judith L., ed. *Psychoanalysis & Women: Contemporary Reappraisals.* Hillsdale, N.J.: The Analytic Press, 1986.

In her introduction Alpert notes that current trends in psychoanalysis include an interest in female development and a growing alliance with feminism. This book is useful for studying the development of women as mothers, especially the chapters "The Gendered Self: A Lost Maternal Legacy" by Susan Spieler and "Some Notes on the Development of Female Gender Role Identity" by Adria Schwartz. See Alpert's essay in the Mothers section, 41.

314. Barnett, Rosalind, and Grace Kay Baruch. "Social Roles, Gender, and Psychological Distress" in Rosalind Barnett, Lois Biener and Grace Baruch, eds. *Gender and Stress.* N.Y.: The Free Press, 1987.

This chapter discusses women's roles as wives and mothers. These roles are looked at in relation to gender differences and the effects of multiple roles on both women and men, such as depression or well-being. Studies as recently as 1968 by Eric Erikson stated that women's roles as a wife and mother were critical to their psychological well-being. The opposite point of view is now believed to be true. See Baruch and Barnett's other works (180, 297).

315. Benjamin, Jessica. "The Bonds of Love: Rational Violence and Erotic Domination." *Feminist Studies* 6: 1 (Spring 1980): 144–174. Reprinted in Hester Eisenstein and Alice Jardine, eds. *The Future of Difference*. Boston: G.K. Hall, 1980, pp. 41–70.

Although primarily concerned with erotic domination, Benjamin looks at the ways males and females differentiate from the mother and how this affects their later relationships. The male is primarily concerned with promoting the self, the female with denying it. Her theories show how the strong feminist-oriented single mother can have a positive effect on her daughter and possibly her son. When the mother is not in a subordinate position and has a sense of herself as separate from her child, she can allow her child both closeness and differentiation. Benjamin stresses the importance of mutual recognition between mother and child, man and woman, but points out the inevitable conflict between one's own desires and the desire to please which can be converted into submission to or domination of the other's will. See *The Bonds of Love* (316) for a more comprehensive discussion of the subject.

316. Benjamin, Jessica. *The Bonds of Love: Psychoanalysis, Feminism and the Problem of Domination*. New York: Pantheon Books, 1988.

Benjamin believes that within the context of all relationships domination is an extension of the bonds of love. One of these primary bonds is, of course, between mother and child. Benjamin traces the structure of domination from this relationship of the child to its mother into adult eroticism and images of the male and female within contemporary society. She feels that mothers who have a strong sense of their own existence as independent from their child and/or mate will be more likely to have egalitarian relationships with their children. She acknowledges the influence of Chodorow (19), Gilligan (324) and Evelyn Fox Keller. This book should be read in conjunction with their works as an important contribution to current psychoanalytical literature on mothering. Benjamin, like Dinnerstein (27) and Chodorow, believes that shared parenting is one solution to current gender problems. She points out, though, that the whole fabric of society must change for shared parenting to be a reality.

317. Chodorow, Nancy. "Feminism and Difference." *Socialist Review* 46 (1979): 51–69. Reprinted as "Gender, Relation and Difference in Psychoanalytic Perspective" in Hester Eisenstein and Alice Jardine, eds. *The Future of Difference*. Boston: G.K. Hall, 1980, pp. 3–18.

A continuation of her analyses in *The Reproduction of Mothering* (19) Chodorow here concentrates on the use of psychoanalysis for the understanding of gender differences. She states that her views of psychoanalysis contrast to those of the French theorists such as Irigaray (115) as well as the Freudian stance of Mitchell (327). Chodorow offers a feminist perspective of "differentiation" (the process by which the infant sees itself as separate from the object world) by which the mother is accorded selfhood. Differentiation is not conceived of as separateness but as a particular way of being connected to others, which can be a healthy basis for mother-child relationships. This is a concise and well-written article which can serve as both a summary and introduction to Chodorow's earlier works (100, 300). This essay has also been published in Chodorow's recent book, *Feminism and Psychoanalytic Theory* (318).

318. Chodorow, Nancy. *Feminism and Psychoanalytic Theory*. New Haven: Yale University Press, 1989.

This newly published collection of Chodorow's essays includes a lengthy introduction as well as two new pieces, one on psychoanalytic feminism and the other a study of early women psychoanalysts. Chodorow defines psychoanalytic feminism as psychoanalysis which is practiced by those who consider themselves to be explicitly feminist. This collection enables the reader to follow Chodorow's theories on mothering and gender from their conception in the early 1970s through a number of significant changes, such as her current belief that the mother is not totally responsible for the development of her child. Other essays in this collection that have been individually annotated include: "Being and Doing: A Cross-Cultural Examination of the

Socialization of Males and Females" (300), "Family Structure and Feminine Personality" (100), "The Fantasy of the Perfect Mother" (21) and "Gender, Relation, and Difference in Psychoanalytic Perspective" (317).

319. Galenson, Eleanor, and Herman Roiphe. "The Pre-Oedipal Relationship of a Mother, Father, and Daughter" in S.H. Kath, A.R. Gurwitt and J.M. Russ, eds. *Father and Child.* Boston: Little, Brown and Company, 1982, pp. 151–162.

This is a study of young girls and their parents. It emphasizes one case history of a girl between 15 months and seven and a half years, which follows her growing identification with both parents. The authors discuss how this particular child's mother repeated a variety of her own childhood experiences through her daughter. However, because the child's erotic attachment to her father interfered with her capacity for maternal identification, she was neither harmed nor benefited from her mother's cathexis. This is a fascinating study, particularly in relation to Alice Miller's (291–293) and Chodorow's works (19, etc.).

320. Gallop, Jane. *The Daughter's Seduction: Feminism and Psychoanalysis.* New York: Cornell University Press, 1982.

The seduction of the daughter refers to the daughter as feminism and the father as psychoanalysis. Gallop looks at contemporary feminist theory in relation to the psychoanalysis of Jacques Lacan. The first chapter is a critique of Mitchell's *Psychoanalysis and Feminism* (327) and the recommendation that anyone interested in modern feminism must read it. The eighth chapter, "The Phallic Mother: Fraudian Analysis," looks at the views of two French theorists on mothers and daughters, Luce Irigaray and Julia Kristeva, who are also concerned with the psychoanalytic theories of Lacan. This complex analysis demands an understanding of contemporary psychoanalysis and Lacanian theory.

321. Gallop, Jane, and Carolyn Burke. "Psychoanalysis and Feminism in France" in Hester Eisenstein and Alice Jardine, eds. *The Future of Difference.* Boston: G.K. Hall, 1980, pp. 106–121.

Gallop and Burke offer a useful introduction to the relationship between French psychoanalytic theory and feminism as well as a comparison between French and American theories which touches on issues concerning mothering, particularly the section by Burke, "Rethinking the Maternal." See Gallop's book, 320.

322. Garner, Shirley N., Claire Kahane and Madelon Sprengnether, eds. *The (M)other Tongue: Essays in Feminist Psychoanalytic Interpretation*. Ithaca, New York: Cornell University Press, 1985.

This book contains three sections: "Feminists on Freud," which includes an excerpt from Gallop's *The Daughter's Seduction* (321) and "The Hand that Rocks the Cradle" by Coppelia Kahn, which is annotated separately (325); "Rereading Patriarchal Texts," which looks at various male writers including Milton and Hawthorne, among others; and "Women Re-writing," which deals with feminist literary criticism, and includes "Writing and Motherhood" by Susan Rubin Suleiman. Suleiman criticizes psychoanalysis as being a theory of childhood without the discourse of the mother. She points out that the concept of the ideally selfless mother held up by psychoanalysis as necessary to the child's development hurts women and prevents their contributions to culture.

323. Gilligan, Carol. "In a Different Voice: Women's Conceptions of Self and of Morality." *Harvard Review* 47: 4 (1977): 481–517. Reprinted in Hester Eisenstein and Alice Jardine, eds. *The Future of Difference*. Boston: G.K. Hall, 1980, pp. 274–317.

Gilligan points out that various male-defined studies show certain desirable characteristics, such as autonomous thinking, to be associated with masculinity. These sex-role stereotypes also stress the separateness of the individual rather than connection to others. She concludes that women's moral judgment develops from an initial focus on survival to a concern with goodness to a belief in non-violence as the means to resolution of conflicts. She follows Lawrence Kohlberg's theory on the stages of moral development, arguing that women go through the same stages, but with different conflicts. Gilligan explored these ideas in greater detail in her book, *A Different Voice* (324), published five years later.

324. Gilligan, Carol. *In a Different Voice: Psychological Theory and Women's Development*. Cambridge, Mass.: Harvard University Press, 1982.

In a Different Voice refers to women's (as opposed to men's) particular ways of thinking about relationships and how these "voices" are reflected in psychological and literary texts. She particularly critiques the male bias in Lawrence Kohlberg's theory of moral development. Gilligan conducted three studies concerning moral issues: "The College Student Study," "The Abortion Decision Study" and "The Rights and Responsibility Study." She points out the difficulties inherent in using certain male-defined concepts in these studies since the female voice speaks from a different kind of morality. Gilligan believes that this female voice is not necessarily related to gender but to ways of making moral decisions which are involved with ethics of care and responsibility for others as opposed to the ethics of survival of the self and the rights of others.

325. Kahn, Coppelia. "The Hand that Rocks the Cradle: Recent Gender Theories and Their Implications" in Shirley Garner, et al., eds. *The (M)other Tongue: Essays in Feminist Psychoanalytic Interpretation*. Ithaca, N.Y.: Cornell University Press, 1985, pp. 72–78.

Kahn looks at the work of Baker Miller (326), Rich (76), Dinnerstein (27) and Chodorow (19), all of whom ask the question, why do women mother? Even if women have other roles and share the responsibility of parenting, they are still usually the primary caretakers, and often want to be. Kahn asks, how does this fact affect gender, i.e., the way in which we define and live our maleness and femaleness? Kahn believes gender is a social rather than a biological product. She states that the institution of motherhood is a root cause for oppression of women because maternal power in the nursery fosters patriarchal power in the world. The nuclear family of the absent father/involved mother perpetuates patriarchy. Kahn believes that it is an important task to look at male identification with the mother as influencing the perception and depiction of women in patriarchal texts. Rich, Miller and Dinnerstein continue Chodorow's theories about child development into adulthood and Kahn relates their work to a basis for reading Freud's accounts of femininity.

326. Miller, Jean Baker. *Toward a New Psychology of Women.* (1976). Boston: Beacon Press, 1986.

Miller, a psychotherapist, looks at the subordinate position of women within male-dominated society from similar positions as Benjamin (316) and Gilligan (324). She uses case studies to illustrate her points and offers positive ways of viewing women's attributes of subservience and nurturance as psychological strengths. Although written in 1976, Miller's work is often referred to in more contemporary writings and is still relevant to women today as a source of inspiration. This edition includes a new foreword in which Miller states that her reasons for writing this book ten years ago are still valid; although she described women's strengths and offered a new image of women, this image still needs to be incorporated into our society. Miller notes the increased violence toward women in the past decade and acknowledges all the new literature on the psychology of women which has been published.

327. Mitchell, Juliet. *Psychoanalysis and Feminism: Freud, Reich, Laing and Women.* New York: Random House, 1974.

Mitchell, a British feminist, attempts to bring the European interest in Freud (Kristeva and Irigaray, among others) to English-speaking feminists, particularly anti-Freudian Americans because she believes that feminists have distorted Freud's analyses. She includes an objective synopsis of Freud's studies on sexuality, respectful critiques of Reich and Laing and incisive criticism of feminists including de Beauvoir (301), Friedan (306) and Firestone (305). Her chapters "The Pre-Oedipal Mother and the Oedipal Father" and "The Holy Family and Femininity" particularly pertain to mothering, but as with Gallop (320), the reader needs an understanding of psychoanalysis.

328. Olivier, Christiane. *Jocasta's Children: The Imprint of the Mother*. (1980). Translated by George Kraig. London and New York: Routledge, 1989.

This work focuses on the effects of contemporary mothering from a feminist-psychoanalytic perspective. After an initial revisionary look at Freud and the oedipus complex, Olivier looks at the differences between men and women, how they are raised to think about themselves and each other, concluding that "men and women live in the same building, but not on the same floor." She then looks at the mother-daughter relationship, particularly in the adolescent years when the daughter rebels against the mother for all the years she has denied her daughter's sexuality. Olivier notes that girls have a choice at puberty as to their next stage of development (whether they accept their female sexuality or deny it, at least for the time being) whereas boys go in a straight line. She thinks, as does Alice Miller (291), that much of our adult life is spent relating to early experiences with our mothers but suggests that women who live *with* their children rather than *through* them will begin to create a generation of young people who will not need to break away from and deny their mothering. Olivier is more accessible than other French theorists, such as Irigaray (115) and Julia Kristeva.

329. Ortner, Sherry. "Father, Mother's Brother, and the Penis: A Review of Juliet Mitchell's Psychoanalysis and Feminism." *Feminist Studies* 2: 2–3 (1975): 167–170.

This review of Mitchell's work (327) says that Mitchell's understanding of Freud's genius is brilliant and was possible because of her feminist commitment to women's history and present situation. Nevertheless, Ortner feels that it is Freud's system which is problematic because if one accepts the premise one must accept the conclusion: the patriarchy. A comprehensive understanding of both Freud and Mitchell is needed for this review.

330. Strouse, Jean, ed. *Women and Analysis: Dialogues on Psychoanalytic Views of Femininity*. New York: Dell, 1974.

Strouse has edited an anthology of classic psychoanalytic texts with contemporary feminist responses. She includes Freud's three essays on femininity, written at the end of his career, which acknowledge differences in the early development of boys and girls, particularly the pre-oedipal period of closeness to the mother.

XI.

Back to the Future: Who's Making the Babies?

This last chapter touches on three areas that relate to issues of mothering in patriarchal society: abortion, surrogacy contracts and reproductive technologies. Each of these issues has produced numerous articles and books on both sides of the question, a few of which have been annotated here.

The consensus is one of concern: concern that women's power over pregnancy and childbirth, the one area in which women *do* have some control, is subtly being eroded. The issue of surrogate mothers poses a particularly difficult problem, similar to that of prostitution and pornography. If we, as feminists, agree that women should have control over their bodies, is it correct to deny the choice of some women to use their bodies for prostitution, for pornography, for surrogacy? The obvious argument is one of exploitation: these activities are all part of a male-dominated social structure wherein men gain "pleasure" from using or looking at women's bodies and men must "father" their own child.

Lori Andrews (331) and Carmel Shalev (349) voice viable opinions in support of surrogacy while other authors such as Martha Field (339) and Alice Henry (343) are more conservative in their qualified support. Phyllis Chesler (333), on the other hand, makes a strong argument against surrogacy in her study of the Baby M case.

Abortion, of course, is not a difficult issue for most feminists as it appears to be the most basic of rights for those of us who will bear and raise the children. Elizabeth Fee and Ruth Finkelstein have written a useful review essay (338) covering three recent books on the subject (including that of Kristin Luker, 345). Two books on the question of abortion written by men have been included: one by David Henry et al. (336) and one by Garrett Hardin (342) in order to show that not all men are irrevocably part of the patriarchy. It is interesting that they both include studies showing the problems encountered by unplanned for children. As for the mothers of these children, recent studies show gains in terms of self-esteem and well-being for teen-agers who have abortions.[1]

But who is benefiting from the new reproductive technologies, asks Gena Corea in *The Mother Machine* (335). This book covers all aspects of these new methods of producing children from artificial insemination to surrogate motherhood and posits that women have the least to gain when men are in control. Corea has also edited an anthology of essays on this subject (334) and other anthologies have been included (see Arditti et al., 332 and Homans 344) in order to give the reader a wide range of the current debate.

Barbara Katz Rothman is a feminist writer who is very concerned with these issues and who has written three books on related subjects (346–348). Sarah Franklin and Maureen McNeil critique one of them, as well as Corea's book and Arditti's anthology, in their review essay (340) on recent books on reproductive technologies. These issues are of extreme importance to the future of mothering in an egalitarian society.

Note

1. Holmes, Steven. "Study of Teen-Agers Hints Gain for Those Having Abortions." *New York Times*, January 25, 1990.

BIBLIOGRAPHY—
ABORTION, SURROGACY AND THE NEW REPRODUCTIVE TECHNOLOGIES

331. Andrews, Lori. *Between Strangers. Surrogate Mothers, Expectant Fathers and Brave New Babies.* New York: Harper & Row, 1989.

Written from a viewpoint supporting surrogacy, Andrews stands in opposition to many of the other authors annotated in this section, with the exception of Shalev (349). She acknowledges that there are many questions surrounding this complex issue but believes that surrogacy furthers reproductive choice, allows women to be "masters" of their own destiny and adds yet another dimension to human experience. She rightly points out that the Baby M case (see 333) had so much attention because it challenged our ideas about the family and caused us to reconsider our closest relationships. She acknowledges Barbara Katz Rothman's (see 346–348) opposition to surrogacy and contrasts her to Carol Pavak, a midwife who served as surrogate mother for three births.

332. Arditti, Rita, Renata Duelli Klein and Shelley Minden, eds. *Test-Tube Women: What Future for Motherhood?* London and Boston: Pandora, 1984.

This book contains 33 essays by a variety of women including Klein, Hammer, Corea and Rothman (see 112, 228, 334–335, 346–348 for other works by these authors). The subjects include sterilization, abortion, disabled mothers (see Birns and Hay, 10 for another work on this subject), test-tube babies, surrogacy, etc., with a final section on "Women taking Control: A Womb of One's Own." Many of the essays include references for further research. Echoing the concerns of Corea, the editors ask how can a woman make free choices in a society where women and people of color are subordinate to white males? They remind us that many women were made infertile by the "old" technologies of Depo-Provera and IUDs and question the interest of male doctors and scientists in helping women bear their own children. See Franklin and McNeil's (340) discussion of this book.

333. Chesler, Phyllis. *The Sacred Bond: The Legacy of Baby M*. New York: Times Books, 1988.

This is the story of Mary Beth Whitehead, the surrogate mother of William and Betsy Stern's child, told from a sympathetic point of view. Much of the book is based on first-hand accounts of other surrogate mothers or mothers forced into "adoption." Chesler is very active in the movement against surrogacy and the book contains accounts of this activity. She sees surrogacy as paid use of the bodies of usually poor or young women by wealthy white people. Appendices include the surrogate parenting agreement between the Sterns and Mary Beth Whitehead and reports by legal and health professionals regarding surrogacy contracts and Whitehead's ability to parent. Mary Beth Whitehead has written her own book, with the help of Loretta Schwartz-Nobel, *A Mother's Story. The Truth About the Baby M Case* (New York: St. Martin's Press, 1989).

334. Corea, Gena, et al. *Man-Made Women: How New Reproductive Technologies Affect Women*. London: Hutchinson, 1985.

This work contains nine essays, including those by Corea (335) and Klein (332), which were originally given at a 1984 conference on women in Holland. They were from a panel concerned with feminist perspectives on the new reproductive technologies, including in vitro fertilization, sex determination, surrogate motherhood and embryo transfer. The consensus was that "test-tube women" are being created at the same time as test-tube babies and that once again women are being exploited by men.

335. Corea, Gena. *The Mother Machine: Reproductive Technologies from Artificial Insemination to Artificial Wombs.* New York: Harper & Row, 1985.

Corea examines the "new" reproductive technologies of artificial insemination, embryo transfer, in vitro fertilization, sex determination and surrogate motherhood as a political issue in order to dispel the myth that they have been developed to help infertile women. She implicates the use of these technologies as a method of social control and political rule. She then offers a historical analysis of each method and states that although advocates of these technologies believe they give women new options and choices that, in fact, can only be true in a society where differences in power and authority do not exist. She also notes that a vast majority of women in in vitro programs have not been helped. In Franklin and McNeil's review (340), they say that "men are reversing the reproductive arrangement provided by biology and constructing a continuous reproductive experience for themselves." This is a provocative book which will be difficult for both men and women, especially those with infertility problems, to read but as Corea says ". . . the issue is not fertility. The issue is the exploitation of women." The book includes a 30-page bibliography. See 334 for another essay by Corea on the subject.

336. David, Henry P., et al., eds. *Born Unwanted: Developmental Effects of Denied Abortion.* New York: Springer Publishing, 1988.

This book includes findings of various longitudinal studies conducted in Czechoslovakia, Northern Finland and Sweden relating to the development of children to whom women gave birth involuntarily due to lack of access or denial of abortions. The major focus is on a study of 220 children born between 1961 and 1963 to women denied abortion twice for the same pregnancy. These children were compared to matched controls from age 9 through 21 to 23. Various tables throughout the book show comparisons which are consistently negative, such as: children are more often born of single parents, placed in foster homes, have parents who divorce before they are 15, undergo more psychiatric consultation, have lower educability and achievement levels (see Hardin, 342, for the same findings). The thesis of this monograph is that unwanted pregnancy leads to a social environment conducive to slightly deviant development in childhood evolving into greater problems in adolescence and early adulthood. It gives the history of abortion and an extensive bibliography on the subject.

337. Donchin, Anne. "The Future of Mothering: Reproductive Technology and Feminist Theory." *Hypatia* 1: 2 (Fall 1986): 121–137.

Donchin explores three alternative perspectives toward recent innovations in reproductive technology: (1) support for the new techniques as a means of achieving a "feminist" future; (2) unilateral opposition, regardless of benefits to individual women and (3) qualified opposition depending on specific threats to women's interests. She then incorporates these viewpoints into current feminist theory, including Firestone (305) and Rich (76), as well as other writers such as Janice Rowland (1984) and Carol McMillian (1982). Donchin concludes that within a social context that is still dominated by male power structures there will be consequences of these technological transformations and if "women's long-term interests are to be represented in determining the future direction of reproductive technology, women will need to participate collectively in shaping public policy." This is one of the better articles this author has found which examines the relationship between mothering and the new reproductive technologies.

338. Fee, Elizabeth, and Ruth Finkelstein. "Abortion: The Politics of Necessity and Choice." A Review Essay. *Feminist Studies* 12: 2 (Summer 1986): 361–373.

This essay looks at three recent scholarly books on abortion to see how these works help to clarify the ethics of abortion and what tools they might provide to help organize people concerned with expanding reproductive rights. The books include: *Abortion and the Politics of Motherhood* by Kristin Luker (Berkeley: University of California, 1984); *Abortion and Woman's Choice:*

The State, Sexuality and Reproductive Freedom by Rosalind Pollack Petchesky (Boston: Northeastern University, 1985) and *Our Right To Choose: Toward a New Ethics of Abortion* by Beverly Wildung Harrison (Boston: Beacon Press, 1983). According to Fee and Finkelstein, Petchesky's book provides a subtle and complex analysis of the abortion issue framed within history and politics and provides a theory for arguing the case of women's social need for abortion. Harrison, who is a professor of Christian ethics, sets out a strong feminist position on the ethics of legal abortion as a social policy. She insists that feminism is a moral argument and that for society to be morally adequate it must encourage the existence of procreative choice. Luker's book (345) describes the emotional truth in the lives of anti-choice women, which the authors see as a main strength of her work. However, they feel that Luker's attempt to isolate the abortion debate from the political process is problematic. The authors provide lengthy and critical reviews of all three books with a coherent analysis of their individual contributions to the question of reproductive rights.

339. Field, Martha A. *Surrogate Motherhood.* Cambridge, Mass.: Harvard University Press, 1988.

Field does not necessarily agree with the concept of surrogacy but has accepted that it is probably here to stay. Her stated aim in this book is to make sense of the legal issues surrounding surrogacy in order to help lay people understand them. The author believes the natural mother should have the right to renounce the surrogacy contract up until the time she gives over the child. Field compares this solution to the legal status of perspective adoptive parents, although in the case of a biological father, Field believes he should have non-custodial rights (accompanied by child support) if he wishes. The book includes extensive notes and a useful bibliography on the subject.

340. Franklin, Sarah, and Maureen McNeil. "Reproductive Futures: Recent Literature and Current Feminist Debates on Reproductive Technologies." A Review Essay. *Feminist Studies* 14: 3 (Fall 1988): 545–559.

Franklin and McNeil point out that reproductive technologies have become part of an extensive debate among feminists because of the social implications these technologies have for women and their connection to more familiar issues such as women's relationship to motherhood, technology and reproductive choice. They have critically reviewed the following three books, all of which have been annotated herein: *The Tentative Pregnancy: Prenatal Diagnosis and the Future of Motherhood* by Barbara Katz Rothman (347), *The Mother Machine: Reproductive Technologies from Artificial Insemination to Artificial Wombs* by Gena Corea (335) and *Test-Tube Women: What Future for Motherhood?* by Rita Arditti, Renata Duelli Klein and Shelley Minden (332). The authors note that Rothman's book is the first major sociological study of amniocentesis. Although it evokes the experiences of women dealing with this technology, the authors feel that Rothman focuses on individual solutions rather than broader social dimensions of the problems raised by amniocentesis. Franklin and McNeil note that Corea's book shows the genre of this procreation story to be recognizably masculine with high stakes in the way of money, fame and power while they found that Arditti's anthology was the most explicitly concerned with the question of feminist resistance. They point out that it is the best known and most widely circulated of these books and was actually instrumental in initiating the current debate. The remainder of the review looks at the issues raised by these books and the continuing debates with which they are linked.

341. Gordon, Linda. "Why Nineteenth-Century Feminists Did Not Support Birth Control and Twentieth-Century Feminists Do: Feminism, Reproduction, and the Family" in Barry Thorne, ed. *Rethinking the Family: Some Feminist Questions*. New York: Longman, 1982, pp. 40–53.

Gordon gives a fascinating history of feminist attitudes toward birth control and abortion as a means of shedding light on changes on these attitudes as well as on the revival of the moral majority in the United States. Today's feminists see birth control as a means of improving women's situations and empowering them with control of their bodies, whereas earlier feminists saw motherhood itself as empowering. Gordon states that feminist goals should be concerned with developing a feminist program and philosophy that defends individual rights while building constructive bonds between individuals. "The feminist reproductive rights movement faces the task of finding a program that equally defends women's individual rights to freedom, including sexual freedom, and the dignity of women's need and capacity for nurturance."

342. Hardin, Garrett. *Mandatory Motherhood: The True Meaning of Right to Life*. Boston: Beacon, 1974.

Published a year after *Roe* vs. *Wade* gave women in the United States the right to abortion, Garrett's small but information-packed book takes a hard look at the pro-life movement and examines the obvious consequences of any right-to-life amendment: mandatory motherhood and the subsequent effect on the children. He includes tables which compare rates of psychiatric consultation, delinquency, public assistance and sub-normal educability for control groups of 120 unwanted and 120 wanted children. In all cases the wanted children showed substantially lower percentages (see David, 336 for the same findings) . The author concludes that abortion legislation that considers the child's right-to-life should also consider the social risk to which an unwanted child will be exposed.

343. Henry, Alice. "Feminists Debate Surrogate Motherhood." Women's Reproductive Rights Campaign, London, England. *Off Our Backs* 15 (April 1985): 12–13.

In the face of tougher government regulations in Great Britain of alternative strategies for infertile women/men, a conference was held by the Women's Reproductive Rights Campaign to debate the feminist viewpoint of surrogate motherhood. This article discusses the concerns voiced at the conference such as ideology, choice, men's involvement, motives and payment. Several comments suggest that women in Britain were in great fear of having their rights with respect to surrogacy and adoption taken away. The author and several of the women's voices heard in this article stress that women should stay together on this issue as it is a "feminist" one.

344. Homans, Hilary, ed. *The Sexual Politics of Reproduction.* Brookfield, Vt.: Gower, 1985.

These nine essays are concerned with the political forces involved in the reproductive issues of self-insemination, contraception, amniocentesis and pregnancy, i.e., with the control of women over their own bodies. Ellen Lewin's chapter "By Design: Reproductive Strategies and the Meaning of Motherhood" looks at women who actively created a resource for themselves by choosing to become mothers as an adaptation to a compromised social status.

345. Luker, Kristin. *Abortion and the Politics of Motherhood.* Berkeley: University of California, 1984.

Luker has interviewed activists on both sides of the abortion issue and shows how these positions relate to broader issues, in particular, the place of motherhood in a woman's life. She examines how chosen lifestyles require validation and support which abortion and right-to-life movements provide. She points out that abortion rights center around two issues: the status of the fetus and the status of motherhood in American society. Pro-choice women see the ability to plan childbearing as essential to fulfilling their potential as human beings through work and parenting while the pro-life women view motherhood as central to the lives of all women. See Fee and Finkelstein's discussion of this book (338).

346. Rothman, Barbara Katz. *In Labor: Women and Power in the Birthplace.* New York: Norton, 1982.

Rothman looks at the politics surrounding prenatal care (i.e., who controls the birthing process and what are their vested interests) with a historical overview. Rothman compares the "medical model" and "mid-wifery model" of birth. She particularly advocates the use of medically trained certified nurse midwives and home births. She also reports on recent advocacy movements to give the mother more rights.

347. Rothman, Barbara Katz. *The Tentative Pregnancy: Prenatal Diagnosis and the Future of Motherhood.* New York: Viking, 1986.

Rothman looks at "selective motherhood," which is not only of whether or not to have children but also what kind of children to have. She sees amniocentesis as dramatically changing pregnancy as well as childbirth and motherhood, often giving women an impossible choice in terms of abortion vs. giving birth to a handicapped child. This book is based on interviews both with women who have received genetic counseling, half of whom decided against having amniocentesis, and the providers of this service. The appendix is a guideline for personal decision making. See Franklin and McNeil's discussion of this book, 340.

348. Rothman, Barbara Katz. *Recreating Motherhood: Ideology and Technology in a Patriarchal Society.* New York: Norton, 1989.

This is an important book that covers a wide range of topics involving mothers and motherhood: the patriarchal mode of family, the Baby M case (see Chesler, 333), technological advances, such as amniocentesis and in vitro fertilization, questions surrounding abortion, surrogacy, adoption and infertility. Rothman sees the need to define a feminist social policy regarding motherhood that takes into account not just the patriarchy but the ideology of capitalism and technology. Like Chesler, Rothman is against the practice of surrogacy.

349. Shalev, Carmel. *Birth Power. The Case for Surrogacy.* New Haven: Yale University Press, 1989.

Shalev, a feminist lawyer from Tel Aviv, offers as her thesis that since men have the right to sell their sperm, subsequently becoming surrogate fathers, so women should have the right to sell their reproductive services. Shalev maintains that surrogacy contracts should be legal, binding and irrevocable. She believes that legalizing surrogacy would have the effect of empowering women since men have tried to deprive women of reproductive choices in order to maintain control of the family within patriarchy (see Andrews, 331). Shalev also believes that the secrecy surrounding surrogacy, adoption and other reproductive means should be ended so that relationships can develop between biological parents and their children.

350. Singer, Peter, and Deane Wells. *Making Babies: The New Science and Ethics of Conception.* New York: C. Scribner's Sons, 1985.

This book looks at cloning, sex determination, surrogate motherhood, genetic engineering and medical innovations in reproductive technologies with the conclusions that these processes should be carefully monitored, if they are to be allowed at all.

351. Whiteford, Linda M., and Marilyn L. Poland, eds. *New Approaches to Human Reproduction: Social and Ethical Dimensions.* Boulder: Westview Press, 1989.

This work looks at the ethics of care during pregnancy, medical treatment of newborns and surrogate mothers. Concerning the latter, six chapters look at related issues including the Baby M case (see 333) and social consequences of technologically assisted fertilization. The editors see the existence of serious ethical dilemmas resulting from the new reproductive technologies, including the rights and responsibilities of various parties.

Author Index

Numbers refer to item numbers except where otherwise indicated.